The Confident Learner

Help Your Child Succeed in School

The Confident Learner

Help Your Child Succeed in School

Marjorie R. Simic • Melinda McClain
Michael Shermis

GRAYSON BERNARD
PUBLISHERS

Family Literacy
Center

Series Editor: Carl B. Smith

Cover art and illustrations by Dave Coverly
Book design by Kathleen McConahay
Cover layout by Addie Seabarkrob

Publisher's Cataloging in Publication
(Prepared by Quality Books, Inc.)

Simic, Marjorie R.
    The confident learner: help your child succeed in
school / Marjorie R. Simic, Melinda McClain, Michael
Shermis.
    p. cm.
    Includes index.
    ISBN 0–9628556–4–2

    1. Education, Primary--Parent participation--Guide-
books. 2. Home and school. I. McClain, Melinda. II.
Shermis, Michael. III. Title.

LB1513.S5   1991   371   91–77793

Grayson Bernard Publishers
223 S. Pete Ellis Drive, Suite 12
P.O. Box 5247
Bloomington, Indiana 47407

About the Authors

Marjorie R. Simic is a former Chapter I teacher and coordinator. She is currently a writer and program evaluator for the Family Literacy Center at Indiana University where she is completing her Ed.S. in Language Education. She has published and made numerous presentations on parent involvement in education.

Melinda McClain is the editorial assistant for the *Parents and Children Together* audio magazine published by the Family Literacy Center and serves as User Services Specialist for the *Parents Sharing Books* program.

Michael Shermis is assistant director of the Family Literacy Center and serves as editor of *Parents and Children Together*, a monthly audio magazine. He also coordinates the *Parents Sharing Books* program, a training program for leaders who teach parents to share books with their children.

Contents

Contents

Acknowledgments

Thanks to the staff at Grayson Bernard for their help, especially Susan Yerolemou for her encouragement and facilitation skills and Kathleen McConahay for her discerning eye with the desktop publishing. The staff at the Family Literacy Center also need to be applauded for their help, including Deborah Edwards, Richard Stewart, Barbara Vultaggio, and Ellie Macfarlane for their proofreading; Kay White for her typing; Lauren Bongiani for her ability to "deal" with the computers; and Jodi Ault, Ruth Fellingham, Beth Fouse, Debbie Booker, and Jamillah Muhammad for other numerous tasks. An extra special thanks goes to Dave Coverly, whose marvelous cartoons add humor to our words, making them come alive.

Marge Simic thanks her family for the support they have given her. Their lessons of encouragement, humor, patience, and unconditional love demonstrate the essence of what families are all about.

Melinda McClain thanks her family for their love, encouragement, and support.

Michael Shermis acknowledges his parents, who have nurtured his ability to be a confident learner and succeed in life.

A Note to Parents

You face several long-lasting challenges during your children's years in school:

- how you can boost your children's levels of self-esteem and motivation
- how you can help the ability of your children to handle stress
- how you can help your children become self-disciplined
- how you can act as strong models
- how you can encourage effective study habits and good health
- how you can work with your children's school.

The following chapters include practical suggestions that you can use right away to make a difference in your children's education at home and at school:

- suggestions for kids who watch too much television

- things to do to help reduce or prevent stress
- ways to encourage children without pressuring them
- ideas for children with learning difficulties
- alternatives to spanking children
- strategies for spending quality time with children.

Each chapter of this book has a set of activities that you and your children can do together. There are activities for fun and learning, for reading and writing, for recreation, for coping with stress, and for motivating children to learn effectively.

Each chapter also has lists of books: books for you to read to find out more about the topic, books for you to read to your children, and books for children to read by themselves. These book lists are divided into age categories: 4–6, 6–8, 8–10.

If you are the kind of person who likes to listen rather than read, these topics are on audio cassettes. Each audio cassette also contains read-along stories which you and your children can listen to together. Information about ordering these audio cassettes can be found at the back of this book.

Now, begin the journey that you and your children can take towards helping them become confident learners and self-reliant individuals who succeed in school.

Introduction:
The Confident Learner

√**W**hat a powerful feeling it is for a child to say: "I can do that!" And then the child does it again and again to reinforce his or her feeling of control and power.

√ "I am valuable. I am competent. I can do that." This is the kind of reassuring self-talk that gives children a sense of confidence. Even the repetition of physical activities, such as bouncing a ball, reflects confidence building. The child is so pleased that he can bounce the ball that he continues to do so.

Parents should promote this evolving feeling of competence and confidence. It is an attitude that leads to independent thinking and problem solving—abilities that help a child succeed in school and in life. However, confidence alone does not bring success; the child must bring skill and hard work to school, as well.

√ But it is important for parents to help their children see that they will be able to manage the world around them. Parents should be the first ones to say: "You did it. I knew you could do it. Way to go!" They should be

involved in helping their children develop a strong sense of self-worth.

√ Building a sense of self-worth is a lifelong pursuit, but the foundation for self-worth is laid in childhood. From those early moments when parents and friends show children how desirable they are, the child begins her march towards success. An individual's sense of success grows gradually, enabling her to feel reasonably secure in moving forward. **That's what we mean by the confident learner—one who has a sense of direction and feels reasonably secure in tackling the learning problems of school and life**.

Self-worth becomes self-confidence when children see that they can indeed achieve a meaningful goal. In various ways, this book elaborates on that idea: how to help children grow in their sense of self-confidence for successful learning. Parents need to communicate their educational expectations, act as models for learning, and praise their children's attempts at learning. This is where confidence starts for most children.

Besides a sense of self-worth, there are other characteristics that help children succeed in school— the desire for school success, the discipline to work on academic tasks, and the knowledge of how to use school resources.

The Desire for School Success

Doesn't everyone want to succeed? Of course they do— in their own way. But some people achieve success by failing. That may sound strange, but the paradox of succeeding through failing is not uncommon. For example, if I know that you will always clean my room for me (even though you say it is my job), I may fail to clean my room so I can succeed in having you do the work. Or if my sports hero was not a success in school, I may follow his pattern of failure in school because I want to be a success in imitating his life. Thus, as long as I achieve my own goal—getting you to clean my room; acting like a star player—I am succeeding even though you may think I am failing.

To determine whether or not I am successful, you have to know what my goals are. If I accomplish what I think is important, I gain confidence in my ability to manage my life. A child's sense of confidence grows through the same process. If she succeeds in achieving those things that seem important, she gains the confidence to tackle future goals in the same way.

Learning goals are no different from other goals in life. If the child has developed confidence in his ability to manage important aspects of my life, he will feel confident in his ability to read, to learn to manipulate numbers, to remember significant facts, to discuss literature, and to solve problems as they are raised in social studies. The key here is to develop a pattern of confident behavior in the child and to establish school learning as a desirable achievement.

Setting Learning Goals

Although it may sound a bit abstract, young children can set goals for learning. Not formally, perhaps, but they are picking up cues from you and from other important people around them. They begin to form expectations for learning from what you say about school and from behaviors that you praise. If you gripe about the dullness of school or about how poorly you performed in school, your children begin to doubt their own ability to achieve in school. They either decide that school is boring or that school is unimportant.

Children will sense that you value learning if, for example, you praise their efforts to read and write coherently or to locate information to solve a problem. In turn, they will push learning up a notch on their own list of priorities. As children get older you can encourage them to set realistic goals for themselves. Help your children to make their goals as explicit as possible by encouraging them to write them down. There is something very powerful about writing goals down on paper. It seems to act like a magnet that pulls children in the direction of the goal. This magnetic force gives them a sense of confidence that reinforces their ability to achieve.

What are realistic learning goals? First, they are goals which are believable to your children. Second, they are goals that are attainable within a given amount of time, perhaps this semester or this year. We are all pleased, of course, when a child says: "When I'm an engineer, I'll build a space ship." The immediate job, however, is for the child to understand third-grade math and to gain competence in multiplying and dividing whole numbers. Gaining these competencies now is one big step toward knowing how to engineer a space ship in the future. Perhaps another immediate goal for this year is to raise the math grade from a "C" to a "B." This may be a realistic goal, whereas moving up to an "A" may not be. Furthermore, if your child wrote an exceptional paper for an English class last year, maybe her goal for this semester could be to write an outstanding science paper, one where she learns something that interests her.

A realistic learning goal, then, is one that your child believes in and feels is achievable this semester or this year. If you write it on a card which is then posted in your child's room or on the refrigerator, the goal statement is more than a reminder; it is a magnet that draws your child toward it. Your praise over the little steps your child takes to achieve that goal adds to the sense of confidence she will feel for learning.

Parents as Model Learners

It is neither necessary nor appropriate to preach to your children about being an energetic learner. The best thing you can do is to show them that *learning is a continuous process*. Show them that learning takes place when you read the newspaper or watch television by commenting on what you learned. When you are faced with a medical problem or have a question about nutrition, make it evident that learning takes place when you are looking for information in a resource book or that you are going to the library for help. If you want to purchase a refrigerator or a car, show your children that collecting consumer information from magazines and writing out comparative lists is a

form of learning. When you decide to increase your income or to enhance your job skills, tell your children that you are attending a seminar on how to better yourself. In other words, if you want your children to value learning, you must show them that learning is important throughout life.

Knowing How to Work

All of us know how to do some things well. We drive well, ride a bike well, spell, type, calculate, repair machines, style hair, clean kitchens, paint, dance—the list is endless. When we perform those things that we do well, we know that we are competent, which in turn, makes us feel confident.

Children need to know how to work and how to act as a learner and as a student in school. Basically, this means they need to know how to get a job done. Some people refer to this as simply knowing how to work effectively. Good heavens! Doesn't everyone know how to work? Not really. One of the most frequent complaints of employers and teachers is that their students and their employees do not know how to work and lack a sense of discipline to make them effective and efficient in their jobs. They do not know how to examine a task, break it down into manageable parts, collect the required tools, and apply them competently to each part.

Knowing how to work results from young children having jobs and from being shown patiently how to tackle the job. Most parents have the experience of saying to their children, "Clean up this messy room. It looks like a tornado touched down in here." Then when we look into the room later, we become angry because the room is still in disarray. Yet our children insist that they have cleaned that room: "See, I hung up my jeans. They're in the closet."

We have a major conflict over cleaning a room for two possible reasons: one, we don't have the same definition of a clean room; and two, our children don't know how to clean the room. Parents can help by showing their children how to break the job into manageable parts: First, hang up your clothes. Second, pick up the stuff that's on the floor. Third, vacuum the floor. You still may not get the room to look like a storefront display, but at least you should notice some improvement.

From the early years, parents should teach their children how to work systematically by giving them jobs that are appropriate for their age. Having a young child put his toys back in a box when he is finished playing with them is a good example. "Put your toys in the toy box and then we'll eat dinner." When it is time to clean house, parents and children can work together to get certain jobs done. "Let's now clean the bathroom. You take the towels to the laundry room and I'll clean the sink. Then you empty the waste basket while I scrub the tub." Through these kinds of cooperative activities early in life, children learn that everyone has to work and that all tasks can be accomplished one by one.

As children grow older, they continue to benefit from having specific chores around the house that are theirs to fulfill. Later, when they are in school, the discipline that they learn from their chores at home will carry over to their responsibilities at school. Just as they learned at home that they have to divide big jobs in order to conquer them, so they will have to apply that discipline to their school work; just as they learned at home that they can't clean the bathroom without cleanser, mops, and sponges, so they will learn that they can't do school work without the use of notebooks, pencils, dictionaries, and encyclopedias; just as they learned at home that the quicker they start a job, the sooner it is finished, they will learn that the quicker school work is started, the sooner it will be finished; just as they learned at home that they will be praised when they complete their chores, so they will be praised for finishing their school work; and, just as they learned at home that others will help them when they don't understand how to do a job, so they will learn that they can get help at school as long as they ask for it.

A Caring Mentor

Developing competence takes practice and it also requires a caring mentor, which is usually the parent. The combination of giving your children appropriate chores, of helping them understand the tasks, and of praising them as they succeed, instills the sense of competence and confidence that they need to succeed in school and in life.

The confident learner is a child who has a positive sense of self-worth, most of which needs to be developed by the family and others who care for the child during his or her early years. These are the formative years when you influence a child by reinforcing: "You can do it! You can walk. You can eat by yourself. You can put on your clothes. You can pick up and put your toys away. You can read that book for me. Nice going! You're a great kid!"

When children hear that kind of encouragement over and over again, they begin to develop a strong self-image and a feeling of empowerment. One of the primary tasks of parenthood is to help children become independent, self-reliant people. Social values also need to be instilled in children, such as caring for other people and for life around us. However, in this book we concentrate on the ways you can nurture your children's individuality so that they can succeed as confident learners.

A caring parent communicates self-worth, the values of learning and independent work, and the strategies for getting things done. The other chapters in this book elaborate on the themes that are important to a child's success in learning—motivation, self-esteem, study, homework, and interactions with teachers and schools. You may find it helpful to write yourself "action notes" on 3" x 5" cards or on Post-it notes to remind you of the strategies or the techniques you will use to help your child become a more confident learner.

Helping Your Child Develop Self-Esteem

When we meet a person who is quietly confident, we usually feel good about that person, probably because he feels good about himself. A friend of mine, Leo, is like that. His attitude seems to say, "I think we can work this out. Let's think about it and get started." Leo's confidence then spreads to me. His attitude shows a self-worth that not only makes him an attractive person, but also gives me a feeling that I can solve problems, too. Leo's self-esteem gives his own life a sense of peace, and it reassures those around him.

Not many people have Leo's ability to make others feel confident just by his presence. But each of us has a feeling of self-worth. That's what gives us the courage to do our jobs, to try new things, and to be responsible for our families. Even if we lack self-confidence and are shy in public, we know deep down that we have value. Parents and friends can be especially helpful in turning our inner feeling of self-worth into an outer expression of self-esteem.

Parents begin building a child's self-esteem when they praise their child's successes, like her first smile, or when she stands or walks. Parents are so thrilled when their children do those things that they make a big fuss. But then they often forget to praise other daily learning that the child shows, like learning to pick up things, to say a new word, to use a spoon, to put on clothes, or to say thank you. Every day a child

learns and does something new that is worthwhile. Parents are the first and most important people who praise and encourage their child. They help their child build her sense of worth with each act of praise.

I know that children can also be irritating. They can be messy, clumsy, noisy, and a lot of work. But parents need to move beyond those problems and regularly build their child's sense of power over the world. This can be done by having a few phrases of praise always ready:

"You learned something new. Good girl."
"You helped your grandma. Thank you."
"You solved that problem. That's great."

Day after day, these words of praise build your child's self-esteem bit by bit. They build the muscles of self-worth in the same way that daily movement builds the muscles that enable us to walk and to work. For the child, there is nothing more powerful than knowing that his parent approves of him and finds daily reasons to show it.

The other great value of praising children's actions daily is that it shapes the parents' thinking. When parents look for the positive things their children do, the parents begin to expect good things from their children. It is certainly true that if we expect good things, more good things happen to us. The more we praise the learning and the helpful things children do, the more they do those kinds of actions. Our statements of praise build self-esteem in children and build a corresponding positive attitude in ourselves.

Learning in School and Self-Esteem

A positive attitude shapes the self-confidence a child needs in order to learn in school. But self-confidence and self-esteem come from more than regular praise by parents; they also come from getting things done in school. Part of school learning is getting work done on a regular basis. Children are rewarded, for example, just by completing a couple of math problems each day. Slowly, they will see they are learning to add, subtract,

3

multiply, and divide. The daily success of doing math activities gives them the confidence to learn more difficult math operations.

√ So parents need to realize that one aspect of self-esteem in school is being able to work when it's time to work. The child who can't get down to work will always feel at odds with the teacher and classmates. Parents can help build good school habits by assigning routine jobs at home, jobs that shape good work habits. For example, have your child pick up the scattered toys and clothes from her room each afternoon before she can have a snack or watch television. Or each

evening after dinner, have your child spend at least 15 minutes reading or doing homework before turning to other things. Then praise your child for finishing those tasks.

√ When children feel that parents are happy with them and that they can finish jobs they have started, it feeds their sense of value. And there is nothing more important for parents to give their children than an expanding sense of self-worth.

Questions about Self-Esteem

All parents have questions and need answers about the academic growth of their children. Here are some questions that parents frequently ask about self-esteem.

> **My own self-esteem isn't very high. Will that affect my child's self-esteem?**

Knowing that your own self-esteem is low may be an important first step in helping you build up your child's sense of worth. Self-esteem is a combination of how we feel about ourselves and how we think others feel about us. Maybe you can recall some things from your childhood that made you feel bad about yourself. For example, perhaps you were called names or were humiliated when you made mistakes. You could share these experiences with your child, if they are not too painful, as a way of saying that we all have to fight against negative arrows that some people shoot at us. At least you can resolve to treat your child differently from the way you were treated.

By learning from your experiences, you can provide your child with a positive home environment. For instance, instead of saying, "You are a bad girl" when your child misbehaves, say: "I didn't like the way you acted in the grocery store. You are capable of acting better than that, and I know you will do better when we go to the store again."

In this way you build up your child's self-esteem by emphasizing the confidence you have in her. Try to notice and comment on achievements that your child

5

makes, even small ones. As you make a conscious effort to build up your child's self-worth, take pride in that achievement, and your own self-esteem will also improve.

⇥ My child is shy. Does that mean he has low self-esteem?

Your child's shyness may be a result of poor self-esteem, but not necessarily. People use the word "shy" in many different ways, to mean easily frightened, bashful, timid, self-conscious, or non-assertive. All of us experience some degree of shyness or anxiety when we have to talk with people we don't know or do unfamiliar things. And some people are naturally less outgoing than others.

One thing you can do is to discuss your child's shyness with him, being careful not to make fun of his feelings. Talk over with him how he feels when he acts shy, and try to find ways that he can overcome his shyness. Is he afraid, for instance? Your child may find a crowd frightening, particularly when people are strangers.

Why not plan together how you will help him the next time he needs to be in a crowd? Being nearby may be enough. Or—if new situations are frightening—work out a way that he can talk with you about his feelings ahead of time and plan what to do. Express confidence that he will act appropriately.

Children do go through stages, and you will see behavior changes. If you feel your child's shyness is lasting too long, causing him to withdraw from other children and adults, you may want to share this concern with your child's teacher or school counselor. Together you can work out a plan to help your child improve his self-esteem.

⟫ If my child has low self-esteem, will it affect her school work?

√ Many studies show that one of the most important factors that influence school success is self-esteem. Children with low self-esteem, even if their intelligence is above average, tend not to enjoy school and easily lose motivation and interest.

Feeling bad about yourself depresses school performance, and, you guessed it, poor performance leads to low self-esteem. This becomes like a merry-go-round, and it becomes harder and harder for a child to jump

off as time passes. As a child falls farther behind, her sense of failure increases, and that certainly interferes with school learning.

If your child gets caught in this failure/low self-esteem circle, discuss remedies with your child's teacher. Perhaps there are programs at school that can give her a boost, or her teacher can arrange appropriate help.

Meanwhile, at home, try to follow some of the suggestions in this book about improving your child's feelings about herself. Punishment, negative reactions, and threats don't build self-esteem. Even a pat on the back and words of encouragement may not be enough. You may need to sit down and help your child with the school work—at least until the cycle of poor performance is reversed—and reassure her that she can do the job and can learn. Express your confidence in her repeatedly, and give praise regularly.

Activities to Increase Self-Esteem

As parents, we are looking for activities that will benefit our children. Here are some activities that help build your child's self-esteem.

Love Pats

Don't wait until your child does something spectacular to show her that she is loved and appreciated. Be sure to give your child hugs, pats, kisses, and lots of compliments all through her childhood.

Mirror, Mirror in My Hand

Hold a small mirror in your hand and repeat: "Mirror, mirror in my hand, tell me why I'm the best grown-up in the land." State two reasons why you are a special person. Then give the mirror to your child and have him repeat: "Mirror, mirror in my hand, tell me why I'm the best child in the land." Allow your child to tell you why he is a special person.

√ What-I-Can-Do Books

Give your child the materials needed to make a simple book—paper, scissors, glue, pencils, crayons. On each page tell him to write and/or draw one thing he does well. The sentences could begin with "I can. . . ."

√ Time Line

Help your child record important times in her life by making a time line. Write important events from her life on index cards and then hang them along a piece of heavy string with paper clips. Hang the time line in your child's room or some place in the house where she will be reminded regularly of the many times she was the central player in the family, starting with her birthday, of course.

√ Proud Chart

Create a "proud chart" on which your child can tape items of which he is proud, like awards, artwork, papers from school, or statements about something he has done well. Add at least one new item each week.

Books for Parents

Your Child's Self-Esteem, by Dorothy Corkille Briggs. Presents techniques to develop feelings of self-worth in children. Offers ideas on self-esteem, discipline, mental growth, and negative feelings.

You and Your Child's Self-Esteem, by James M. Harris. Provides advice to assist parents in helping their children establish positive self-images. The relationship of self-esteem to handicaps, divorce, and discipline are some of the topics discussed.

Self-Esteem: A Family Affair, by Jean Illsley Clarke. Gives examples of different types of families, along with suggestions to help the adults in each family unit build their self-esteem and their children's. Provides worksheets, family exercises, and parenting tips.

Books to Read Together

Ages 4–6

The Me I See, by Barbara Shook Hazen. Looking at his own physical features can help a child understand his uniqueness. Rhymed verses and pictures present and explain the different parts of a child's body.

Saturday I Ran Away, by Susan Pearson. Emily is the littlest in her family, and she is tired of it. So, she decides to run away. While she is getting ready to leave, she discovers that the other people in her family would like to run away too. After she arrives at her destination, one by one, the rest of her family comes too!

Ages 6–8

The Wednesday Surprise, by Eve Bunting. Anna and her grandmother have a surprise for Anna's father. They are creating a birthday present for him. Even though Anna is only seven, she is teaching her grandmother to read! They spring the surprise on the family at the birthday party.

Annabelle Swift, Kindergartner, by Amy Schwartz. Annabelle goes to her first day of kindergarten feeling very confident because her older sister has given her some tips on what to do. The advice isn't very good, but Annabelle's self-confidence makes her day a success.

Ages 8–10

Tiffky Doofky, by William Steig. Tiffky Doofky enjoys his job as a trash collector, and his work is always done well. Because he is so modest and hard working, the beautiful Estrella falls in love with him.

Boy, Was I Mad!, by Kathryn Hitte. The boy in this story is so mad he decides to run away from home. On his way he gets a ride in a wagon, pets a few dogs, and plays in the park. After doing different things he enjoys, he finds out he is no longer mad and returns home. He is glad he went back home, and so is his mother.

Books for Children to Read by Themselves

Ages 4–6

Sunshine, by Jan Ormerod. The sun wakes up a young girl, who then wakes up her daddy. She gets herself prepared for the day, and is the only one who is ready on time.

11

I See, by Rachel Isadora. Pictures of the things in a young child's life are shown with easy sentences describing each page. Familiar objects and pictures are used for this short book.

Ages 6–8

Isadora, by Jody Silver. A lovely donkey named Isadora buys a red boa for herself. She likes the boa, but she will not wear it because she is afraid of what the other animals will think. One day she gathers enough self-confidence to wear the boa, and it makes her feel good about herself.

Ira Sleeps Over, by Bernard Waber. Reggie invites Ira to stay overnight with him. Ira worries that Reggie will make fun of him if he brings his teddy bear. At bedtime, Ira is surprised to find out that Reggie sleeps with a teddy, too, and returns home to get his.

Ages 8–10

Pamela Camel, by Bill Peet. Pamela isn't being treated very well at the circus. She is small and clumsy, and the people at the circus think she is dumb. After she stops a train from crashing, she becomes famous, and the circus trainers realize how smart she is.

Herbert Hated Being Small, by Karla Kuskin. Are you too short? Herbert thinks he is, until he meets Philomel. She thinks she is too tall. After they become friends, they both decide that being short or tall depends upon how you look at things.

2

How to Motivate Your Child

Everyone uses the word *motivation,* but most of us don't think much about what it actually means. We know that motivation has something to do with getting us moving toward important goals. We know that some things seem easy to do because they appeal to us, or we think there is going to be a big reward. Other things are not very interesting, even though they may seem important to our friends, children, or bosses. Why is one person, for example, motivated to learn all the details of baseball while another doesn't care if a baseball game is ever played again? That question is at the root of what we call motivation.

In order for a person to be motivated, it is clear that the end result must be worth the effort. If we want our children to be motivated about school, then learning in school has to be important to them; learning school subjects has to be one of their goals. To move toward a goal, two things have to happen: first, we have to have a clear goal that appeals to us; and second, we have to see that there is a way we can attain that goal. One appealing goal might be to learn to find factual information on our own. And we can see ourselves in the reference section of the library with the skill to use dozens of major reference books.

Parents and teachers have the tough job of helping children set goals and of seeing the steps it takes to achieve them. For example, how can we get a seven-year-old second grader to find information (How long does a cat live?) or to learn math facts (6x3=18)? This kind of learning is narrow in focus but has long-range importance because it develops skills that will serve children throughout their lives. You as parents can see the value and purpose of these activities. The question is how do we motivate children to work on them when they can't see the long-range value of learning facts and of developing study habits? Now we begin to sense why motivating young children to do academic tasks is often difficult for us.

So how do we do it? Here are four steps you can take to motivate your children.

Step 1: Be a model of curiosity.

Children naturally look to important adults in their lives as models of what they should do. They want to please and to imitate important adults. Obviously, parents and teachers are important adults to them.

That means if you want your children to work hard on school subjects, you have to demonstrate in your life that school learning is important. You have to seek answers in books, show curiosity about math facts, or indicate that it is important to you to learn what is going on in society and in government, for example, in order to vote wisely.

You can do those things by asking questions out loud and then asking out loud how you can find the answers, "I wonder if there is a way for me to learn how to use a computer? I could look in the newspaper

for an ad that might give me information." Then you can pursue answers in newspapers or encyclopedias or call the library for help. There are all kinds of ways of demonstrating to your children that you are curious about the world and new knowledge. This helps your children want to achieve similar attitudes and skills themselves.

Step 2: Praise and reward efforts to learn. Mostly children want to please their parents and their teachers. They will respond well when those important adults praise them and occasionally reward them for their efforts. When your children ask questions and pursue answers by looking them up in the dictionary, newspaper, or magazine, you ought to say: "Hey, that's a smart idea. Now you're thinking. You're going to do well if you keep that up."

When your child talks about what is going on in school, you can show interest and enthusiasm for what the child is learning. Naturally you want to praise a child when she is making progress. That doesn't mean waiting until the child brings home a paper with an "A" on it. If a teacher says your child is doing better this week than last week or better this report period than the last report period, that's a time for rejoicing at home. Then you can say, "Way to go! Now you're working. I'm sure glad to see that you are improving. That's just great!"

Step 3: Solve real problems.

One of the best ways to motivate a child to do school work is to show that it has application outside of school. For example, can we parents show that reading stories enriches our emotional lives? Can we demonstrate that math is used regularly in our shopping, our check writing, and our measuring to buy paint for our walls? Can we find information in newspapers and magazines that helps us decide how to vote, how to plan a trip, or how to solve a health problem? It takes effort and attention to those kinds of details for us to help children see that what they are doing in school will pay off in life. It's all part of a well-known principle in psychology: the more visible and real we can make something, the more likely it is that we will achieve it.

Step 4: Lay out the steps to success.

We said that the goal has to be visible. It's even more important that the means to achieve the goal are clear and concrete. One of the reasons many of us don't achieve our dreams is that we have no sense of how to move from where we are now, toward the dream.

I can remember one little third-grade boy writing about his dream to be a professional basketball player like Magic Johnson. In his composition he said that all of his friends, teachers, and parents thought that he would never be like Magic Johnson because he was too clumsy and not fast enough. He said that it was awful when no one believed him. Wouldn't it have been wonderful if some of those people had given him some

direction? Wouldn't it have been uplifting for that child if his parent had said: "If you are going to be like Magic Johnson, you are going to have to learn to run fast and to shoot well. Why don't you start by shooting baskets after school every afternoon or by getting on a local Boys' Club track team to run faster?" By giving him steps to take, the parent would have allowed the boy to keep his dream at a point in his life when encouragement and support were so important.

Motivation for children is not just interest, and it is not gimmicks that simply catch their attention. Motivation means focusing on a goal and laying out clear steps needed to achieve that goal. Parents play an extremely important role in helping children become motivated for school work. So, first, be a model of curiosity for your children. Second, praise and reward them for their efforts to learn. Third, help your children solve practical problems according to what they have learned in school. And finally, always help your children take the first little steps that lead them to bigger goals. Then you'll be surprised at how motivated your children will be in school.

Questions about Motivation

All parents have questions and need answers about the academic growth of their children. Here are some questions that parents frequently ask about how to motivate their children.

> ❧ **I don't know what is wrong with my child. She is not interested in school and doesn't care if she does well or not. What can I do to get her interested in improving?**

Have you asked your child why she does not care about school? Parents and children need to share what goes on at school as well as what goes on at home while they are away. Your child needs to know that you are interested in her—what problems she may be having at school as well as things that may be bothering her at home. I would encourage you and your child to meet with your child's teacher to discuss this lack of self-motivation. Sometimes lack of motivation can stem from your child's lack of self-worth—a feeling of not being adequate or good enough to fulfill expectations. It may be fear of failure.

Don't let any problems—school or home—spoil your child's chances of success. Meet non-success head-on. Find out what it is that may be causing this lack of interest and then work with how to replace this failure with success.

❯ How can I motivate my child without always having to give him rewards and presents?

If you have not started the habit of rewarding with material prizes—don't! Changing established habits is sometimes difficult, but it is possible. I have found with my own children that when they have met with success, a simple statement acknowledging their achievement, like "I bet that really made you feel proud," can bring self-satisfaction to my children. They are able to reflect and respond to how they felt— "I really felt great" or "You're right, that made me feel proud." These are healthy ways to express and share pride without material rewards.

I think the best rewards that you can give are yourself, your time, and your attention. Kind words, hugs and pats on the back, an extra story at night, a walk in the park, extra time allowed for a bike ride or even a bike ride to a new area, allowing 30 minutes more for TV watching one night, relieving your child of a chore for one week—the possibilities are endless.

❯ My child does well in school, but does not like school because she says it is boring. Do you have any suggestions for me so I can help her?

Children sometimes say they are bored because it is the "cool" or the "right" thing to say, when actually they really do like school. Some children are bored by choice. If your child expects something is going to be boring, then it probably will be boring. Encourage your child to become engaged in what is going on and to make an effort to be interested in whatever is at hand. As adults, we know that not all work is entertaining.

Your child may feel that she already knows about the things that are being discussed in class. Encourage her to extend herself—develop a sense of inquiry, curiosity, and discovery beyond what she may think she already knows. Ask her to act interested and see if that doesn't relieve her boredom. Schedule a conference with your child's teacher and your child together so that your effort at home is reinforced at school.

Activities for Reading and Writing

As parents, we are looking for activities that will benefit our children. Here are some activities that help your child look ahead to long range outcomes.

Time Passages

At the beginning of each month, make a calendar for your child to keep track of her daily reading time.

Decide on a minimum time you want your child to read each day, either to you or to herself. Each day that she reads for the allotted time, allow her to color in the square for that day or place a sticker in it. Decide on a reward system based on a certain number of days, number of days in a row, or the total days in a month. Save the calendar pages so your child can see her reading time. After doing this for several months, your child may develop a habit of daily reading.

Stick to It

Help your child stick to reading by rewarding him with a sticker each time he reads a book. Make a booklet out of paper similarly to trading stamp books. The child can see how many books he has read by counting the stickers. Set up a plan for redeeming the stickers for prizes. For example, 10 stickers and the child can stay up past his bedtime; 20 stickers and he can invite a friend to go swimming.

Scavenger Hunt

Encourage your child to finish a book. Look through a book before your child reads it, and make a list of objects for younger readers to find and a list of words or phrases for older readers. For very young children who cannot find words for objects, draw the object or cut it out of an old magazine or catalog. After they find all of the objects, words, or phrases, they will have read a book and completed the hunt.

Raffle Reading

Adults and children can participate in this family raffle. Each time a whole book or 50 pages are read, a family member writes down her name, number of pages read, and the book title. Place this record in a jar or box. Explain to your children that the more books they read, the more chances they have to win the raffle. Decide on a prize beforehand; then once a month hold a drawing to pick a winner. For example, the winner can choose a favorite dinner or dessert, relief from a chore, or the place for the next family outing.

Books for Parents

The following four books are suggested to help you motivate your child.

Raising Children to Achieve, by Eric W. Johnson. Based on psychologist David McClelland's achievement motivation, the author gives parents and teachers methods for developing children's motivation to achieve. Each chapter also includes family games and exercises.

Raising Kids Who Love to Learn, by Children's Television Workshop. Presents the four stages of learning, along with practical ways to encourage a child's yearning to learn. Gives child-focused home activities and provides ideas on how to play and interact with your child to help him achieve without feeling pushed or pressured.

Help! for Parents of Children 6 to 12 Years, by Jean Illsley Clarke. Gives answers to child-raising problems written by parents, for parents. Gives background information about developmental stages, and practical suggestions. Also listed are additional resources for parents.

Books to Read Together

Ages 4–6

The Very Busy Spider, by Eric Carle. A spider is invited to take part in a variety of activities by several different animals. She refuses so that she can use the time to build her nest. Her efforts pay off when she catches a fly to eat. The web in the book can be felt because raised print is used.

Ages 6–8

The Art Lesson, by Tomie dePaola. Tommy wants to be an artist when he grows up. For him to create his own art at school, he has to make a deal with his art teacher. Tommy works everything out and grows up to be a terrific artist.

Ages 8–10

Miss Rumphius, by Barbara Cooney. When Miss Rumphius is a young child, her grandfather instructs her to try to make the world a more beautiful place no matter what else she does when she grows older. She lives out her dreams and then is able to make the world more beautiful by planting lupines.

Books for Children to Read by Themselves

Ages 4–6

All by Myself, by Mercer Mayer. The critter in this book can do lots of things all by himself. He can brush his fur, get dressed, and help take care of his sister without any help. But when it is time for bed, he needs his parents to read him a bedtime story.

Ages 6–8

Max, by Rachel Isadora. Max is a terrific baseball player. He discovers a way to become even better. Max goes to his sister's dancing class to warm up before each game. His method must work because he hits a home run!

Louanne Pig in the Talent Show, by Nancy Carlson. Louanne's friends are all getting ready for the talent show. She is grumpy and does not want to try because she does not think she has any talent. Then when George loses his voice, Louanne gets to be the master of ceremonies and decides she likes talent shows after all.

3

Stress Affects Your Child's Learning

Can you remember facing a test for which you were not well prepared? Most of us remember having those feelings. Our bodies tensed up and our minds seemed to forget even the things we thought we knew. Some of us struggled through those tests with great frustration, feeling that we had failed or, at best, had done poorly. Others of us were so fearful of the consequences that we tried to cheat. We slipped notes inside our shirt sleeves or peeked at our neighbor's paper.

Formal tests in school often bring on stressful feelings. But we and our children are tested everyday. When the teacher calls on us to give answers or to explain our thoughts, there is pressure to perform. Some people react so negatively to those opportunities to perform in public that they freeze and refuse to respond. In their minds it is better to get a poor grade than to submit one's ideas to public ridicule.

But those pressure-filled situations are not limited to school. Adult life, too, brings us face-to-face with pressures that can raise our blood pressure and cause us to act in negative ways. A complaining customer, or a row of figures that doesn't balance, or a boss who always seems to breathe down our necks are

a few examples of situations that can lead us to act negatively. A friend of mine, for instance, thought that his boss and his fellow workers were always criticizing him. As a result, he wrecked a bulldozer and quit a good-paying job. He said there was too much stress there for him to survive.

What causes stress? We do.

School, jobs, the family, our friends, and the news media all put pressure on us. They all ask us to perform, to give public evidence that we can do our jobs and can live responsible lives. But that's just normal daily pressure. Everyone faces daily pressure. How we react to that pressure determines our stress level. In other words, the feeling of stress, the feeling of fear or panic is a feeling that we create ourselves. Evidence for the truth of this statement can be found in the ways that different people react to the same moment of pressure. In class, some children will collapse in a jumble of tears when faced with a test. Others will tackle the test with energy and self-confidence. Same test. Same external pressure. But very different kinds of reactions and very different levels of stress.

It is not always clear why some children rise to meet the pressures of school while others freeze or do a poor job. Unwise parents may try to shield their children from all external pressure, then children may never learn how to handle it. Other parents may expect too much of their children. They may expect their children to perform far beyond their abilities, thus pressuring them to do things that they cannot perform well. Or children may sense extreme anxiety in their parents when the parents feel their children will not measure up to others. That usually means that the parent is afraid of being embarrassed because the child is not a star. Yes, a parent can actually exert pressure that the child does not know how to handle. Therefore, the child builds stress and fear that work against good performance.

We don't want to imply that parents are the only cause of stressful reactions in their children. All sorts of pain, illness, ridicule from other children, and other emotional strains may lead your child to see almost any pressure as more than he or she can stand. Moving

29

to a new school, divorce, being excluded from a popular group, an abusive relative—all kinds of negative events can make a child vulnerable and less able to deal with other daily pressures. Thus the child creates within himself a level of stress for these daily pressures that is inappropriate and hurtful.

In other words, anything that adds pressure to the child or to the parent creates an opportunity for the individual to build stress so that it hinders performance instead of helping performance. As the world changes at a faster and faster pace, each of us gets pressure from more and more segments of our life. Our jobs change; we move; we hear about war; we read about competition with other countries; we argue with a neighbor about our space; we fear we won't make a team or get a promotion; we fear the environment isn't safe: all kinds of events and worries in modern life add to the pressures on us and on our children. You can see, then, how easy it is for us to turn those many different pressures into a growing sense of stress.

Signs of Stress in Children

To help your child deal with stress, first learn to recognize its signs. For example, some children withdraw from activities they previously enjoyed; some refuse to respond or to interact with others; some begin to act like little children again; some blame others for all their problems—other children, the teacher, bad light in the classroom, and so on. Some children begin to fear everything associated with school and may even be unable to board the school bus or may have a fit of anger about going to school. In some children, feelings of stress provoke physical symptoms: headaches, stomach cramps, vomiting, bed wetting, frequent nightmares, and so on.

These signs of stress in children should be taken seriously because they can lead to continuing problems in school and in the child's attitude toward life.

Here are some of the things that you can do to reduce or prevent stress:

First, tell your child that you have noticed that something is bothering her. Children need to know that someone recognizes that they have a problem and that you care enough to work on it.

Second, try to put as much order in your child's school life as you can. A sense of order helps develop a sense of control, a sense of competency. Provide a place for study, for example, where books, paper, and pen are handy. Then help your child set aside specific

times for school work. The same kind of orderliness in other aspects of life may also be helpful. This means that meals, chores, entertainment, and bedtime may need to be planned with a degree of regularity, so the child begins to gain control over himself through the orderliness of his environment.

Third, give your child regular encouragement about the things that he does well. Praise his efforts and remind him that most competence comes from many repetitions. He can reduce stressful feelings by talking with you or a teacher about pressure and ways to reduce it. People can learn to reduce their feelings of stress.

Fourth, help your child build friendships that will support him. Encourage your child to invite friends to the house, people who will enjoy similar activities and who will boost your child's self-esteem.

Fifth, be a good listener. Give your child a chance to express his or her feelings. You may want to say: "You look like you've had a bad day. Do you want to talk about it?" Then help your child define the problem.

Sixth, hugs and signs of affection are always beneficial.

Seventh, try to reassure your child that all children have pressures and fears. He is not alone. It is important for your child to realize that he can gain control of most of his feelings by realizing that they are *his* feelings. Therefore, he should not blame other people or the circumstances for his anxiety. With your help, and perhaps the help of teachers and other professionals, he can learn to control any negative, stressful feelings that he has.

As you work with your children, please treat their fears and anxieties with respect. They are real fears to your children, and those feelings may in fact hinder school work and make friendships difficult. You can't fight your children's battles, but you can act as an ally, and you can enlist teachers or counselors in the battle as well.

Each of us has our own strengths and weaknesses. As much as possible, focus on your child's strengths. Offer praise and encouragement so your child will see that through his strengths he can build self-esteem and reduce harmful stress. In the same light, recognize your child's weaknesses and do not demand that your child do things that will only disappoint both of you.

When it is helpful, remind your children that pressures in life can be used to either stimulate the effort needed to succeed or to build fears and anxieties. How they respond is up to the individual. Together, you and your children can learn to respond in healthy, positive ways to pressures that we all feel.

Questions about Stress and School

All parents have questions and need answers about their children. Here are some questions that other parents have asked concerning stress.

> **My son becomes very upset when he thinks he doesn't know something. Often he remarks that "the other kids are smarter than I am." What can we do to build his confidence and help him overcome this anxiety?**

Kids change so quickly they sometimes forget how much they have learned. As a parent, you can help your son build self-esteem by pointing out all the new things he does know.

You might get out an old favorite book and say, "Remember when you had trouble reading this book?" Or if your child is struggling with long division, say, "Remember when you couldn't even add 6 plus 9?"

Many children who experience difficulty learning are subjected to harsh words or are criticized by parents, teachers, and peers. Many of these youngsters develop feelings of anxiety because they sense they have no control over what happens to them during learning. To make matters worse, many of these children feel guilty and are emotionally upset because they think they have let their parents or teachers down.

Before positive changes can occur, you and your son must become aware of the problems that are causing the stress and anxiety. Talk with your son about school. Be sure to ask your son what he likes about school or what he thinks he is good at. Share with your son things you think he does well. Talk about the things that he would like to improve or things he is having trouble with at school—classmates, assignments, teachers, or activities outside of school. Discuss with your son ways he can deal with the things that are upsetting to him. Let him know that he does not have to face his problems alone.

It may be necessary to share your son's anxieties about school with his teacher. The teacher's role is crucial in creating an instructional environment that leads to your child's success.

Explain to your son that learning does involve some degree of stress; even adults feel tension when they are confronted with unfamiliar things. Parents and teachers cannot always prevent stress, but they can help a child to cope when it occurs.

Encourage him to ask for help when he doesn't understand something or to reread directions and information that are not clear to him. Provide the kind of support at home that will help your son become confident. Take time each evening to discuss things that have happened at school. Become involved in the homework that your son brings home. Offer praise for the things your child has accomplished, and provide support when your child is having difficulty.

We all feel encouraged when we realize we are making progress. A few minutes spent talking with your son about his accomplishments can build the self-esteem and confidence that are necessary for success in school.

> **I don't like sending my children to school in a hurried, frantic way. Getting them all off to school, packing lunches, getting breakfast, finishing forgotten homework, making sure they have everything they need on time can**

**be very stressful for all of us. What can we
do to reduce that "morning rush hour?"**

In many homes, the morning scene looks like
something from "America's Funniest Home Videos!"
Kids (and even some parents) fly out the door, eating
their breakfast as they run for the bus. Papers fly out
of the backpacks or don't even make it into the backpacks!

Let's face it, not all of us are morning people. But
children do need to learn to get to places on time and
to be ready to go to work. Here are some suggestions
for eliminating morning "rush hour" at your house:

First, help your children establish good habits.
Make sure they hang up their coats as they walk in the

door. Give each child a place to keep boots, hats, gloves, and school bags so they are easy to find the next morning. Second, schedule a regular homework time, and establish a regular bedtime. Kids who zonk out on the couch watching a TV program at 11:00 can't rise or shine the next morning. Third, help your children learn to be responsible for getting themselves up in the morning. Provide an alarm clock for each bedroom. It may help to set everyone's alarm clock 15 minutes earlier. Even a few extra minutes can make a real difference. Creating a sense of order is a good way to start.

Fourth, a successful morning begins at night. Before your children go to bed, have them lay out everything they will need for school. This is a good time to make sure everyone has lunch money, homework, and any permission slips that require parent signatures for field trips. Also, have them select the clothes they will wear the next day.

Oh, by the way, before everyone leaves, take a second to say, "I love you" and "Have a good day" to each child. Nothing will get their day . . . and yours . . . off to a better start.

> **Our daughter has some learning difficulties. I sometimes feel this contributes to her difficulty in making friends. How can we support her in getting through some of these difficult times?**

The pressure to be accepted and liked by others is felt by all children, typical or not. However, the special child often has more difficulty in establishing friendships and therefore has a greater chance of feeling left out. Some special children attend schools or programs outside of the neighborhood, which makes the task of making friends even more difficult. Feelings of rejection or exclusion, combined with not living up to expectations at school, can all build up and contribute to unhealthy stressful feelings.

Having a friend—someone with whom you can share confidences or enjoy similar pastime—creates a feeling of self-worth that can reduce school stress. Help your daughter make friends by encouraging her to invite children to your home. It is worth the extra effort on your part.

➢ I want our children to do well in school. How can I encourage them to do their best without putting too much pressure on them to excel in school?

A recent national survey asked children about their biggest worry. Kids said it is the intense pressure to do well in school. Twenty-four percent of the young people said that "doing well" in school and in sports is what they worry about most.

We want to support our children's desire to do well, but we may need to rethink the kinds of messages we give them. For instance:

When you watch your children in athletic events, do you criticize their performance afterwards? Or do you try to focus on the fun of participating in the event?

What happens when your children bring home a test? Do you first talk about the questions they got wrong? Or do you look for what they got right or did well?

How about when your children help you with a job around the house? Do you emphasize the things they need to do better? Or do you thank them for their help and talk about one thing they did especially well?

Have conversations with your children that support what they are doing in school and in other activities. Focus on your children's strengths—what they have accomplished—rather than on what they have not been able to do successfully. Take every genuine opportunity to praise their efforts. This positive approach will show your children that you appreciate the good things they do. There is no better way to keep them sailing ahead on an even keel.

❯ I like going over the papers and tests my daughter brings home from school, but she doesn't like doing this. Should I push this?

Your daughter can learn a lot from a test or an assignment—even after it's graded and handed back. A test can show where she had difficulty and, perhaps, why. This is especially important in subjects or skills that build on earlier learning. For example, kids who can't multiply and divide won't be able to understand fractions.

When your daughter brings home a graded test paper, sit down and discuss it. Talk about the right answers as well as the wrong answers. Praise your daughter for what she has done well. When you see a wrong answer, ask your child to explain why she answered as she did. Sometimes children know the right answer, but express it incorrectly. Other times, they may need to review some material.

It helps to talk about how well your daughter used her time during the test. Did she finish? If so, suggest that she spend some time after she finishes to check her work. Did guessing help? Helping children learn to take tests builds confidence for the next time. Going over work in this way helps your daughter establish study habits that can help her when she works independently.

Finally, look to see what the teacher has written on the test paper. Are there any suggestions for improvement? If you have any questions, be sure to contact your daughter's teacher.

Activities to Help Cope with Stress

Use some of the following activities to help your child learn how to deal with stress.

Wise Exercise

Exercise increases the heart rate and stimulates the circulatory system, which helps the body reduce the effects of stress naturally. If you or your child are feeling pressured, upset, sad, or angry, try going for a long, brisk walk, or doing some aerobic exercises.

Funny Medicine

"Laughter is the best medicine" may be an old saying, but there is truth in it. When you laugh, chemicals are released in your body that help you feel more relaxed. When life gets hectic, take time to watch a funny slapstick comedy or read some comics or a joke book with your children and have a good belly-laugh together.

Count to Ten
Help your child learn to control himself. When reacting to stressful situations, teach her to close her eyes and count slowly to ten before she says or does anything.

Let It Out
Being able to express our feelings can sometimes reduce the stress that we feel. You can encourage your child to talk to you, or to someone else he trusts, about what is bothering him. Or suggest that he write down his feelings and thoughts in a diary.

Books for Parents

Books to Help Children Cope with Separation and Loss, by Joanne E. Bernstein. Offers ideas on using books to help children cope with death, divorce, separation, desertion, serious illness, war and displacement, foster care, stepparents, adoption, homelessness, new sibling, new school, and new neighborhood. Gives an extensive list of books with description, reading level, and interest level. Includes a list of resources for adults.

The Divorce Workbook: A Guide for Kids and Families, by Sally Blakeslee Ives and others. A workbook to help children express and explore their fears and feelings about divorce by reading, writing, talking, and drawing. Covers marriage, separation, divorce, emotions, and ways children can help themselves cope. Explains the "legal stuff" such as custody, child support, and visitation.

Helping Children Cope with Stress, by Avis Brenner. Describes the range of stresses children face and gives different strategies to help them cope. Topics include childhood stress; one-parent, two-parent, and multi-parent families; separation; death; adoption; divorce; physical, sexual, and emotional abuse; neglect; and living with an alcoholic parent.

Books to Read Together

Ages 4–6

Where Is Daddy? The Story of Divorce, by Beth Goff. Janeydear lived in her house with her daddy, mommy, and her dog named Funny. Then her parents get a divorce and Janeydear becomes sad and upset. Her parents help her to understand, and she learns to be happy again.

Everett Anderson's Goodbye, by Lucille Clifton. Everett Anderson is struggling through the different stages of grief after his father dies. Everett comes to understand that even though his father is gone, his father's love will always be with him.

Ages 6–8

Everett Anderson's Nine Month Long, by Lucille Clifton. First Everett's mom marries Mr. Perry, and now they are going to have a new baby in their family. Everett is a little wary about having a new brother or sister, until Evelyn arrives and fills their home with joy.

How Many Stars in the Sky? by Lenny Hort. Mama's away one night, and her son cannot sleep. Then the boy finds that his daddy hasn't been able to sleep either. Together they set off into the night on a journey of discovery.

Ages 8–10

The Washout, by Carol Carrick. When a summer storm washes out the road, Christopher and his dog Ben row across the lake for help. Christopher stays calm in the face of danger and manages to survive and find help.

Annie and the Old One, by Miska Miles. Annie tries to make time stand still so that her aged grandmother will not die. She eventually comes to understand that life and death are both part of an ongoing cycle.

Books for Children to Read by Themselves

Ages 4–6

When the New Baby Comes, I'm Moving Out, by Martha Alexander. A young child does not like the idea of a new baby coming to his house to live. He does not want to share his things or his family. After his mother shows him how much he means to her and explains the neat things a "big brother" gets to do, he decides a new baby will be terrific.

Ages 6–8

Harriet's Recital, by Nancy Carlson. Harriet loves her ballet class, but hates the thought of a recital. She overcomes her stage fright, dances well, and enjoys the recital.

Horace, by Holly Keller. Horace has spots and all the members of his adopted family have stripes. After searching for a family who look just like him, Horace decides that being part of a family depends on how you feel, not how you look.

Ages 8–10

The Berenstain Bears' Moving Day, by Stan and Jan
Berenstain. The bear family decides to move
from their cozy cave home to a new house in the
valley. Brother Bear isn't sure if he will be happy
and feels anxious about the move. Then they
move in, and the new house becomes their home.

The Sorely Trying Day, by Russell and Lillian Hoban.
Father comes home after having a bad day and
discovers Mother is also having a bad day, because of the poor behavior of the children and
their pets. They all make up and feel much better
afterward.

Discipline and Learning

As a parent you've been in those conversations that are filled with questions like these:

> How do you get your child to behave?
> What kind of discipline should I use?
> Should I spank my child when she really
> gets out of line?

Knowing how to discipline children is not something that is straightforward and easy. But there are some guidelines that we can use to help us. The founder of the Montessori Schools, Maria Montessori, had this to say about discipline:

> We call an individual disciplined when he is
> master of himself, and can, therefore, regulate

his own conduct when it shall become necessary to follow some rule of life.

That phrase, "master of himself," may be the key to giving us direction in this matter of discipline. Some people quite obviously are not masters of themselves. Recently I met such a person in a train station. I was waiting to catch a morning train when a young man in his twenties started talking to me about all sorts of unconnected things. As I wandered to the coffee machine, and then the train schedule, even to the restroom, this young man followed and talked. In other words, he became a nuisance.

I still had thirty minutes until my train was leaving and I was sure that this young man was going to prevent me from reading my paper with his constant chatter. Then a policeman approached us and said to the young man: "I've seen you around here before, haven't I? Todd right? Are you harassing this man?"

"No," he replied. "Just talking."

"Have you got yourself straightened out?" the policeman asked. "Are you following your program? Are you taking your medicine? What are you going to do today to make yourself useful?"

Since I did not want to embarrass Todd, I walked away while they finished their conversation. And I thought about the positive way the policeman handled the situation. He was dealing with a known nuisance, but he did not muscle him out of the building or tell him to get moving. He talked to the fellow and asked him about his life and what he was doing to improve it. What an excellent example of dignified discipline in a public place. And he made my life more pleasant in the process.

That train station scene shows most of the elements that parents face with their children. Their child misbehaves or doesn't follow the rules or hurts someone. Adult intervention is needed, both for the benefit of the public and that of the child. In former times, most parents might have settled such a problem with a hard swat on the child's rear. Discipline was often equated with punishment and humiliation. But today there is a move away from this kind of punishment. Some studies show that physical punishment often leads to anger and defiance and doesn't necessarily make the child a more responsible citizen.

Thus we return to Montessori's phrase, "master of himself." How can we help children become masters of themselves? A spanking certainly gets the child's attention quickly, but in the long run, we want the child to learn to govern his own actions. But how do we help inexperienced children accomplish that end?

One general guideline ought to be that we treat our children in the way that we want to be treated. That golden rule is a helpful guide. Think about the times that you might have been disciplined for your actions—you were late for work, made a rude comment, shouted at a fellow worker in anger, or accidentally broke a piece of equipment. Those things happen because we are human and sometimes forget to be nice. When they happen, you don't expect to be slammed across your backside so hard that you topple over. Nor do you expect to be stood in a corner.

As an adult you suffer the consequences of your "misbehavior." You lose an hour's pay; your colleague ignores you; you don't get a promotion, and so on. If you are wise, you analyze the situation that led to those unhappy consequences and you make a plan to change your behavior. The key word here is "consequences." You want to change your behavior because the consequences of misbehaving are unpleasant or cost you money, not because you were punished physically.

How, then, do we help children focus on the consequences of their actions, so they can see that misbehaving leads to consequences that are not in their best interests? Here are some suggestions from an approach called "discipline with dignity":

1. Establish clear rules.
2. Have fair limits with consequences for misbehavior.
3. Work with the child to develop a plan to change.

Establishing clear rules is probably the most difficult aspect of effective discipline. These rules could be written and posted on a bulletin board, or on the refrigerator. On one classroom bulletin board, for example, I saw these rules: no hitting, no stealing, no throwing objects, no defying authority, no abusive language, and no continuous disruptive behavior. Those rules are simple yet clear, and they cover a wide range of potential problems. That same set could be easily modified for use around the home: no hitting, no lying, no taking someone's things, no leaving big messes, no abusive language, no continuous disruptive behavior.

Having fair limits, with consequences for misbehaving, is the next step in setting up effective discipline. While an important part of any approach to behavior is to praise the child when she behaves well, it is also important to know when to step in when she misbehaves. Every child misbehaves, that is, throws a temper tantrum, hurts others, breaks things, creates noise when she should be quiet, and so on. Children have short attention spans and often forget. They are rambunctious and let their natural energy explode, sometimes in disruptive ways. Parents have to decide when their children's behavior has gone over the limit. Usually that point is reached when the child has been reminded or admonished but continues to do things that interfere with someone else's well-being or threaten her own safety. That's the point at which the child sees consequences that are unpleasant to her.

The next step in this approach is to have the child come up with a plan or a statement that describes how he will change. Whether spoken to the parent or written down, the idea is that the child learns to make decisions about his own behavior. The child takes responsibility for learning what good behavior is. The child has to think about why it is not appropriate to hit his sister and to make a statement about what he will do the next time in a similar situation.

This thoughtful approach to discipline expresses confidence in children and also shows that we parents expect our children to be responsible for their own behavior. This approach doesn't relieve the parent of responsibility. The parent has a more thoughtful role than ever. Parents have the difficult job of clarifying the rules, of showing that there are high expectations, and of taking the time to work with their children in becoming responsible. Those things are accomplished through praise of good behavior and by calling time-out when the rules have been broken.

What does this have to do with learning? A lot! Learning is primarily self-discipline. The person who knows how to control her behavior is then free to concentrate on other things. She can concentrate on the subjects to be learned for instance. When we discipline ourselves to do our expected daily work, we are free from the tensions and hassles that result when we allow distractions, such as undone tasks, to get in the way. A child who learns self-discipline has a great advantage in learning at school and at home.

Remember to help your child in the following ways:

1. Be clear in your expectations. Don't say, "Clean your room." Rather say: "Pick up your clothes;

put the dirty clothes in the hamper; and vacuum the floor."

2. Be considerate. Especially remember to praise your child for the kind of behavior you expect. Hugs and pats of affection can supplement words of praise.

3. Express your beliefs. Let your children know how you feel and provide constructive guidance. Remember the policeman who asked the young man what useful activity he was going to do?

4. Point out consequences so your children see that they are making a choice. "If you keep making that noise, you will have to sit in the 'time-out' place for ten minutes." Then, be sure to follow through.

5. Listen attentively to what your child has to say. Instead of issuing a judgment about bad behavior, have your child account for his behavior by asking him, "Please explain why you did that?"

6. Communicate with your child instead of giving him or her a sermon. Discuss her behavior instead of preaching at her.

When all is said and done, you might want to recall this paragraph written by a young man who was asked why he felt he had succeeded in college. He wrote:

> My parents know all my faults, but to hear them talk (and in my presence, no less) you would think I have few equals. They show me in a hundred ways that they approve of me. When I disappointed them, they never showed anger, but instead assured me that they knew I would do better next time, that I could do great things. Everyone should have one person somewhere in his life like my parents.

May your children write a similar paragraph about you one day.

Questions about Discipline

Most parents have questions concerning their children's behavior. Here are answers to a few of those questions, and some suggestions you can use.

➢ **My child will obey me at home, but she has problems behaving in school. Is this normal? What should I do?**

Misbehavior at school is a problem if it interferes with your child's learning and the learning of other children around her. You may want to remind your daughter of the importance of good behavior and how it affects her success at school. If you know which actions in school are causing problems, discuss them with your child. Discuss the different kinds of behavior that are expected at home and at school. A conversation with the teacher may provide possible reasons for your child's misbehavior.

The differences in rules and guidelines may be confusing or difficult for your daughter to handle. School requires more self-discipline from our children because of the number of students in a classroom and the fact that the teacher can't possibly watch everything that goes on. Your daughter may need opportunities to learn self-discipline at home that can help her in school. Instead of your telling her exactly what she can or can't do and then checking up on her, let her exercise some responsibility for making decisions within the limits you have set. For example you might say, "You can go outside to play with your friends for awhile, but I want your homework completed and your clothes picked up off the floor before dinner." You have

given her limits and expectations, but she has the responsibility for completing certain tasks and some freedom as to when to do them. You may also want to work out a joint plan with the teacher.

⌗ Do you have any alternatives to whipping a child to control behavior?

There are lots of ways we can teach our children discipline without having to use physical punishment. More positive ways of reminding children of their misbehavior can be:

- isolating them, which means sending them to their room or a room away from others. For a small child, a particular chair may be used as a 'time-out' chair.
- taking a privilege away from them. For instance, no TV for an evening or a week.
- asking them to apologize to the person they have offended.
- making them give back what they have taken.
- making them pay for the damages they have caused out of their own pocket, or maybe having them do work in exchange for the damage they have done.
- grounding them. This means placing restrictions on their activities outside the home for a specified time. Be sure to stick to your restrictions.

When giving punishment, remember, first, make the punishment fit the crime. Some behavior problems merit no TV for one day; others may merit no TV for three days.

Second, be consistent. Don't reward a behavior one time and then ignore it or punish your child for it the next time. This confuses your child.

Third, don't make threats or promises that you can't keep. Keep your promises. For example, if you tell your child she can go to the park when her room is cleaned, stick to it.

> **I have tried to let my son make decisions for himself in certain situations. Now he wants to make all of his own decisions. This is a problem sometimes. What should I do?**

In trying to allow our children a voice and an opportunity to make decisions, we sometimes create problems for ourselves. Parents want their children to make decisions, but may have a hard time giving up certain kinds of authority. Also, in allowing our children decision-making privileges, we must also realize that they can't have a say in every instance. For example, you may allow your child to spend money from a piggy bank that is his, but drawing money from a savings account set aside for his college education is definitely out of the question.

You need to consider your child's maturity in decision-making. These considerations require you to set guidelines on where you draw the line for your child's decision-making. You will need to provide reasonable explanations. "Because I said so" or "because I'm the parent" probably isn't going to be a good enough reason to satisfy the child who is challenging you about making his own decisions.

Don't make it seem as though there are sides in the issue—an adult against a child. Instead, explain that you are looking out for your child's needs and what is best for him in the long-run. When your son does make decisions, you must remember to respect them. This will help him learn to respect your decision.

Activities for Fun and Learning

One way to build a better relationship with your children is to do fun things with them. Here are a few fun activities to try.

Picture That

Give your child crayons and paper so she can draw pictures of the story you are reading or telling her. The drawing will help her visualize the story. Talk about the pictures and ask her questions such as, "Now what are they doing?" "Then what happened?"

Dolls, Bears, and Books

When your young child wants to read a book to you and you are too busy, help him set up an audience. Gather several dolls and stuffed animals to listen to him read a book. Arrange them around him or in front of him so

that they will be able to "see" the pictures. He will be reading to his favorite friends, and you will have time to finish what you are doing.

A-B-C Inventory

Let your children choose the room they want to use for this game. Have them write down the objects in the room in alphabetical order by the beginning letter. Whoever finds items for all twenty-six letters wins the game. You may want to skip q and x.

$%&@%¢ U%$$0#%$ (Secret Messages)

If your child does not enjoy writing letters, suggest sending messages in a secret code. Your local library will have books explaining codes written just for children. Check out a couple of these books and let your child decide on a secret code to use. From secret codes, you might be able to develop an interest in reading some spy novels or mysteries. Be sure to read how to decode as well as code messages.

Books for Parents

The following resources may help answer your questions about your child's behavior and discipline:

The Difficult Child, by Stanley Turecki and Leslie Tonner. This step-by-step approach shows parents how to: understand their child's behavior, respond to conflict situations, lessen the strain on the family unit, discipline and manage their child, cope with the special demands of infants, and find support from others.

Disciplining Your Preschooler and Feeling Good about It, by Mitch Golant and Susan K. Golant. Presents ideas for parents on how to discipline their children with love. Topics include tantrums and lying, family meetings, positive reinforcement, setting limits, parental expectations, and logical consequences and follow through.

How to Discipline with Love, by Dr. Fitzhugh Dodson. A practical guide that shows how love and discipline go hand in hand in parenting. Addresses spanking, problem-solving techniques, communication, authority, family council, and the difference between discipline and punishment.

How to Talk So Kids Will Listen. . .and Listen So Kids Will Talk, by Adele Faber and Elaine Mazlish (audio cassette). Suggests ways to avoid turning simple conversations into arguments; to instruct rather than criticize when you correct your child's behavior; and to find effective alternatives to punishment.

Books to Read Together

Ages 4–6

Richard Scarry's Please and Thank You Book, by Richard Scarry. The animals in this book show how pleasant results can come from using good manners. Includes stories about parties, safety, cooperation, family, and friends.

The Tale of Peter Rabbit, by Beatrix Potter. Peter is told not to go to Mr. McGregor's garden, but he goes anyway. He has several close calls and a narrow escape. Upon returning home, he does not feel well and must take his medicine then go straight to bed.

Ages 6–8

The Berenstain Bears Forget Their Manners, by Stan and Jan Berenstain. Mama Bear notices the family has forgotten their manners. Even though the cubs do not like Mama's idea, they soon begin using good manners and find it makes things go much more smoothly.

The Tale of Squirrel Nutkin, by Beatrix Potter. This is a tale about a tail that belongs to a sassy squirrel named Nutkin. Old Mr. Brown puts up with Nutkin's riddles for awhile, but then the little squirrel pushes the owl too far, and almost ends up as his snack.

Ages 8–10

Phoebe's Revolt, by Natalie Babbitt. Phoebe demands that she be allowed to wear her father's clothes, and not her own, which have lace, frills, fluff, and bows. Her father grants the wish, but Phoebe soon changes her mind, and her clothes. A funny portrait of childhood rebellion.

Miss Nelson Has a Field Day, by James Marshall. The Smedley Tornadoes cannot win a football game. At practice the team just goofs off . . . until "The Swamp" arrives, and whips them into shape. The team learns that hard work can have big rewards, but still can't guess who Viola Swamp really is.

Books for Children to Read by Themselves

Ages 4–6

I Can, by Christopher Neal. Amy wants to learn to ride her new bicycle, but she is afraid because she continues to have accidents. Suzie and Mrs. Biddle

introduce Amy to the "Can Do Can." She becomes confident and learns to ride her bike well.

The Manners Book, by June Behrens. Chris and his bear, Ned, show how to use good manners in different daily situations. They discuss please, thank you, excuse me, introductions, helping, and sharing.

Ages 6–8

The Butter Battle Book, by Dr. Seuss. The Zooks and the Yooks can't get along with each other because they do not butter their bread the same way. A great war evolves between the two groups, until finally they both invent a bomb. But who will use it first?

Lyle and the Birthday Party, by Bernard Waber. Lovable, good-natured Lyle the crocodile tries very hard to help with Joshua's party, and even to have a good time. But envy gets the best of him.

He becomes so mean with jealousy that he ends up feeling sick because of his bad behavior. Lyle begins to feel better when he helps others and stops thinking so much about himself.

Ages 8–10

The Berenstain Bears: No Girls Allowed, by Stan and Jan Berenstain. Brother and his boy cub friends try to exclude girl cubs from their club. Papa and Mama help Sister learn that it won't help the situation to try to get revenge, and they come up with a better plan.

So What If I'm a Sore Loser? by Barbara Williams. Maurice thinks Blake is a sore loser every time he beats him at something. Then when Blake beats Maurice at working a jigsaw puzzle, Maurice says Blake is a sore winner. What is worse than a sore loser? A sore winner!

Parents as Models

Not too long ago, I asked a group of parents at a PTA meeting to describe a good parent. Their answers pointed out some of the ways that parents do make a difference. None of the answers involved providing material things. All of them grew out of caring for children and spending time with them. Here's a partial list.

Good parents:

- can smile after only a few hours' sleep.
- put love notes in lunch boxes.
- are there when needed, out of the way when not—and are able to recognize the difference.
- laugh at knock-knock jokes. (Even the zillionth time.)
- soften discipline with kindness.

- accept that a child may not turn out exactly as they please.
- know that children can't be perfect.
- celebrate special moments, no matter how small.
- tell their kids they love them. A lot!

From the very beginning of their lives, children imitate others. They imitate much of what they see and hear. Most parents are unaware of their role as prime models. But when parents "show" how much they love and care for their children, children can only benefit in positive ways because their self-esteem rises and they will imitate that love and care.

We are also models for our children, for instance, when we face problems. Consider the following situation: A mother finds her preschool daughter angrily taking a book from another child and then sees her slap the other child's arm. The mother furiously jerks her daughter by the arm and starts shaking her, yelling, "I'll teach you to play rough!" This mother is unknowingly modeling the very behavior that she wants to discourage in her daughter.

How could the mother have handled this situation differently? She could have stepped in and said, "I know you want her book, honey, but you must not hurt your friend. Give the book back to her and tell her you are sorry for hurting her. Ask her if you can borrow it after she has finished with it.

Then I'll help you find something to do while you're waiting for your turn."

This approach makes it clear that hurtful behavior is not allowed, and it also gives the child a positive way to deal with her need. Most importantly, it shows the child that she can rely on her mother for advice when she needs it. Our children need to know that they can trust us for help, for care, and for love. Remember, to be a model means to create an image of behavior in the minds of our children.

√ Even though we may not be teachers, we parents can do a lot to help our children succeed in school. Here are some ways that you can create images in your child's mind that will help with school:

1. Read. Take time to read. When you read books, magazines, and newspapers, you show your child that reading is valuable. Important adults like Mom and Dad do it all the time.

2. Write. Write notes to your child. Have your child help write grocery lists. Let your child see you write a letter to a friend or to your parents. Then ask your child to enclose a note of her own.

3. Show interest. When you show interest in your children's school work, they sense that you care and that you want them to do well. It only takes a minute at a meal to ask what interesting or important things happened today in school, and then a few minutes to listen to the answers.

4. Show curiosity. Show your curiosity by asking your child to teach you something she learned that day. Also, develop an interest in learning something new yourself. Everyone is a learner—that's the image you want to leave with your child.

5. Show patience. Keep calm and be helpful when things don't go well, for example, when your son doesn't think he will be able to get his report done on time or screams, "I hate math" when he can't figure out a problem. Sit down with him and say calmly: "Let's go through this thing step by step. Maybe we'll be able to work it out."

The point of these examples is to remind you of the many opportunities you have to act as a model for learning and literacy. These small actions on your part make it more likely that your children will do well in school.

√ As we become more aware of how we influence our children, we can examine ways of changing our own behavior so that it is more in line with the beliefs and values that we want to pass on to our children.

Of course, no one can be a perfect model all the time, and often we act in ways that we would rather not have our children imitate. The way we choose to respond to our own imperfections, however, provides an example for our children. It's worth admitting to our children the mistakes we make.

There certainly are no surefire answers that will produce predictable results when it comes to raising children. As parents we make decisions each day based on specific situations, on what we already know about our children, and on what we desire our relationships with them to be like. By realizing that we are models for our children, we can adopt a more deliberate attitude in shaping what our children learn and eventually how they feel about themselves.

Questions about Parenting

Most parents have questions concerning their children's behavior. We would like to answer a few questions and offer some suggestions to help you be a good model for your children.

> **I realize now as a young, single parent that school and learning are much more important than I realized when I was growing up. I want my children to get a good education. How can I help my children value school and learning?**

The high dropout rate is proof that many kids do not see the value of school. Most children are not likely to fall for the old line, "Well, I want you to do better than I did." You want the best for your children, of course. Probably the best thing you can do is to get involved in learning yourself. That's your best strategy for convincing your children to keep learning.

Actions really do speak louder than words. Why not make this the year you go back to school or take a short course on a hobby that interests you? Many school districts or community colleges offer a wide variety of courses. Perhaps you can learn a new skill, a new language, or become certified or licensed in a new area. Check your local library. It may offer opportunities for adults to become members of reading clubs that meet regularly to discuss books. You may prefer to organize your own adult reading group. Seek out friends and neighbors who would be interested in meeting on a regular basis to exchange and discuss books.

You can show your interest in learning by studying with your children. Pick something appealing and become an expert on the topic. Read books, magazines, or watch TV shows about the topic. Listen to audio programs and attend demonstrations on your topic. Then share the information and learn from one another. Some schools organize "Parents Sharing Books" clubs. Perhaps you'll want to participate.

Talk about your educational goals with your children. Not only are you showing your children that you enjoy reading and learning new things, but you benefit when you identify the goals you are trying to achieve. You will show your children that "education is like a golden key that will unlock so many more doors to our future."

➢ **My daughter's teacher has asked for parent volunteers. I don't know if this is something I want to do, but I would do it if it would help my child. What are the benefits of parents volunteering in the classroom?**

Parent volunteers listen to students read. They give make-up spelling tests. They work with individuals while the teacher works with a group. School volunteers can offer the school a variety of skills and talents. I know of one parent who became a volunteer for the simple reason that she wanted to see her own child at work in school. The parent thought she would try it for a week or two. But after only one week, the parent saw the importance of what she was doing. Volunteers learn at least as much as they teach! This particular parent couldn't believe how many different ways the letter E could be printed, pencils could be held, or patience could be tried!

By volunteering, you show children that you value learning and are willing to help others learn. Besides that, volunteers can give each child some special attention. Students have more actual reading time and less time listening passively. But most of all, this parent found that volunteering was fun. She was helping children learn. Each week she saw children improve, learn more, go farther, or take another step.

You don't need special skills to be a parent volunteer. All you need is time. Some parents feel they have to volunteer for a whole day or half a day, but teachers appreciate whatever time you have to offer. It is important that you and the teacher work out a convenient time for both of you. Once parents have signed up to volunteer, teachers count on them. Canceling out at the last minute may put the teacher in a bind. Being a responsible and considerate parent volunteer makes for good parent-teacher relations.

If you have some concerns about being a volunteer, share some of these concerns with your child's teacher or the school principal. Let the school know you are willing to try it on a temporary basis. Maybe you would feel more comfortable working in a classroom other than your child's. These things can be worked out with the school. It is important that you enjoy your time at school so you can share this valuable experience with your child.

> **Between work and school, it is difficult for our family to spend much time together. What can we do to emphasize the importance of family and spending quality time together.**

It may be impossible to share every evening meal with the entire family present, but try setting one night aside when everyone sits down to the meal together. Your family can work their schedules around to make it a special event. Use this evening meal to share what is going on in your lives. Setting aside an evening to be together at the dinner table shows your children that making the extra effort to be together is worth it—that family is important. You might make it an occasion to use the good dishes or special placements, or have flowers or candles on the table. Block out the evening so no one feels rushed. Everyone can pitch in and help so this special event does not become one more chore for mom. Remember, the food does not have to be fancy; it is the company that counts.

Maybe your family can benefit from other activities to improve interaction. Set up a family savings account. Everyone can save for a special project or trip that the entire family can enjoy. An event you work hard to take part in usually means more. Build something, like a tree house, a doghouse, or a birdhouse. We all enjoy making something ourselves, and it is extra special when it involves team work. Or take on a family service project. Children need role models for learning the importance of doing things for others. Choose an organization—a nursing home, church, hospital, or school—and donate your time together. Plant a garden or turn yard work into something the whole family does together. It is an ongoing project that shows children about responsibility. Something as simple as taking walks can be done together as a family. It costs nothing, and it is great exercise for the entire family.

Being a family is something we must work at in order to preserve it. You and your family can learn together that life has many things to offer and sharing them as a family can be beneficial to all members—both adults and children.

Be a Model in Practical Ways

Here are some practical ways that you can be a daily model for your children. Read through the ones listed below and select a couple that would be best to try with your family.

Prime Time

Be selective in your television viewing. Decide what you would like to watch instead of spending the evening staring at the screen, watching whatever happens to

be on that night. Your children will learn that there are choices in television viewing, and one choice is to turn it off and do something else.

Read All about It

Take your children to the library and help them select their books, but also make a point to choose something for yourself to read. Let your children see that reading is important to you and enjoyable.

Hit Me

Play cards or board games with your children for family fun. You can be a model of good sportsmanship and show them how to play for the fun of it without having to always win.

What a Deal

Before buying a car or other expensive household items, include your children in researching the product and finding the best price. They will learn how to be wise buyers from watching and helping you with your purchase.

Books for Parents

Parents, Please Don't Sit on Your Kids: A Parent's Guide to Nonpunitive Discipline, by Clare Cherry. It is easy to convey the wrong message to our children without meaning to. The author discusses how parents tell little white lies to their children, such as "I don't want to talk to her. Tell her I'm taking a bath," or "Don't tell Daddy we were in this store. I don't want him to know what I bought." These statements show children that it is okay to lie. We can hardly fault them later on when they lie to us, if we have been giving them this message all along. The way we conduct ourselves in ordinary everyday situations conveys our values to our children much more clearly than lengthy explanations. There is truth in the old saying, "Actions speak louder than words."

How to Generate Values in Young Children, by Sue Spayth Riley. A father promises his son, Randy, that he could spend his first allowance as he wished. Randy enjoys the powerful feeling of authority as he looks around the toy store, but his father becomes impatient and suggests several toys to him, hoping to hurry him up. Randy finally decides on some bubble gum, and his father immediately lectures him about how candy is bad for the teeth. Randy then chooses a water pistol, and his father points out how it is cheap and won't last an hour. "Why don't you save your money till next week, and then you'll have more to spend?" says the father. "But Daddy, I want to spend my allowance now, and I really do want the

bubble gum. And besides, you said I could decide. . ." And so runs the dialogue between Randy and his father until finally Randy decides on the fire engine that he didn't want very much, and his father is relieved that the ordeal is over.

Randy was being cheated of a very valuable learning experience. Naturally, Randy's father was right about bubble gum being bad for the teeth and cheap toys breaking easily. He probably was concerned about conveying to his son the value of being responsible. But this is something that Randy needs to learn from his own experiences, not only from his father. Instead of showing Randy that he respects his right to choose, his father is modeling for him an authoritarian style of parenting. Randy is not learning to be responsible, but to blindly submit to a higher authority. Rather than learning to trust himself and to feel confident, he is learning that he is not capable of making important decisions. How would Randy benefit if his father would provide him with lots of opportunities to make choices? As Riley points out, practice in the process of choosing helps to develop decision-making ability, insight, flexibility, and the imagination to cope with the loftier choices that come later in life.

Playing Smart: A Parent's Guide to Enriching, Offbeat Learning Activities for Ages 4 to 14, by Susan K. Perry. Hundreds of things for parents and children to do together—from photography to cooking. Shows how to find adventure in ordinary places close to home and how to turn spare time into quality time.

Your Child at Play, by Marilyn Segal and Don Adcock. Presents ways to support children in their physical, intellectual, and social development through play activities. Special sections focus on conversational play, discovery play, creative play, and playing with friends.

Books to Read Together

Ages 4–6

Parents, by Carme Sole Vendrell and J.M. Parramo. Shows the role of parents in raising and caring for their children. Contains a section with practical tips for parents.

Mothers Can Do Anything, by Joe Lasker. Looks at several possible occupations which can be held by a mother. Suggests many non-traditional jobs, such as judge, doctor, dentist, plumber, and chemist.

Ages 6–8

My Dad Takes Care of Me, by Patricia Quinlan. Luke feels strange because his dad is the one who takes care of him. He begins to realize how nice it is to have his dad at home and enjoys being cared for by his father.

The Not-So-Wicked Stepmother, by Lizi Boyd. Hessie does not want to stay with her daddy and his new wife for the summer. She thinks her stepmother will be mean and that she will have a horrible vacation. Hessie finds out stepmothers aren't always wicked, and they become friends.

Ages 8–10

Ramona and Her Mother, by Beverly Cleary. Mrs. Quimby goes back to working full time and Ramona feels unloved and abandoned. Ramona wonders if anyone will ever pay attention to her again.

Ramona and Her Father, by Beverly Cleary. Mr. Quimby just lost his job, Beezus is grumpy, Mrs. Quimby is busy working, and even the family cat is grouchy. Ramona tries everything to cheer her family up and make life better for them.

Books for Children to Read by Themselves

Ages 4–6

Family, by Helen Oxenbury. Looks at the various members of a family. Shows a picture of the person and gives the word that identifies their title in the family; for example, mom, dad, baby, sister.

Grandma and Grandpa, by Helen Oxenbury. A little girl goes to visit her Grandparents each weekend. They sing, play dress-up, house, and hospital, until Grandma and Grandpa become so tired, they need a nap!

Ages 6–8

Jafta's Mother, by Hugh Lewin. Jafta is a little boy living in South Africa. He tells about his relationship with his mother, his love for her, and the day-to-day life in his village.

Jafta's Father, by Hugh Lewin. Jafta's father works in the city during the winter. Jafta remembers the fun they have shared in the past, and looks forward to his father's return to the village in the spring.

Ages 8–10

The Mommy Exchange, by Amy Hest. Jason and Jessica decide to switch moms and homes for the weekend. After one night, they are ready to end their mommy exchange. They realize that their own moms and homes are best for them.

Uncle Willie and the Soup Kitchen, by DyAnne DiSalvo-Ryan. A boy spends the day helping his Uncle Willie work in the soup kitchen. He learns he can make a difference in people's lives by helping to fix food for the hungry people in his neighborhood.

6

Homework Is Home Learning

Homework is back in style. It used to be standard procedure for children to have daily homework assignments; then, as educational winds shifted, homework lost favor. Now we parents realize that we need practice and learning at home to develop abilities that enrich our children's lives. Some subjects, such as reading and math, require lots of extra practice, and the home is the best place for it.

√ So what does this mean for parents? Helping children to work on their own at home isn't easy. TV, games, and neighbors pull children in directions that look much more inviting than does studying at home. On their own, children do not usually see the long-term value of practicing math and communication skills. Why should they read history or try to figure out why electricity runs the motors in their homes? Nintendo games and hanging out around the TV set are much more fun. So parents have to help their children look into the future to see the value of homework and home learning.

As is the case with so many attitudes, children take their first cues from their parents. If parents see homework as worthwhile, then it's likely their children will value it also. If parents see that home study and home practice lead to competent performance in reading or science, then children will take on that same vision. And if parents believe that their children must accept responsibility for their own success as learners, then children will gradually accept responsibility for their own progress.

Specific things that parents can do to help with home study include the following:

1. Listen, read, and talk with your children about school work. Just showing interest will improve their grades.

2. Provide structure to make home study easier to perform. For example, you can do the following:

    *   Work with your children to set aside a specific time each day for homework.

    *   Answer your children's questions and ask them about the material they are studying, but do not do their homework for them.

    *   Encourage your children to bring home class notes so they become part of preparation for home learning.

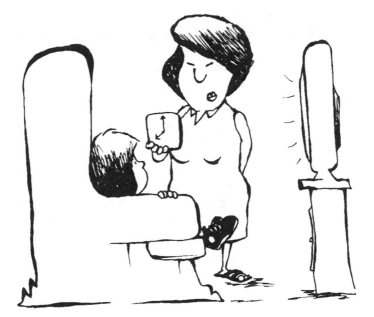

√• Expect homework every night, even though your children may have an occasional free night. Reading an interesting book is a good substitute for assigned homework.

√• Encourage your children to write notes and ideas as a way of promoting critical thinking.

For more on notetaking, see our comments in the question-and-answer section of this issue.

√3. Allow flexibility in time and place for home study, but encourage your child not to cancel it, or give it such a low priority that it becomes meaningless. If your child has an important game to play or some other school-related activity during normal study hours, allow her to shift homework times in order to participate in these other valuable activities. Homework can be done before or after the activity—preferably before.

√4. When your child completes his homework, ask him to talk about what he has done or what he has learned. A brief overview helps you keep abreast of the things your child learns in school and alerts you to problems he may be having. If you ask for this information each evening at a specified time, it is easier for you to keep track of your child, and it also puts a time cap on the homework period. Your child will probably appreciate that.

5. When your child is studying for a test, discourage "cramming" the night before the test. Ask your child to bring a textbook home at least every other night the week before the test. She can teach you what she has learned in school. Reverse roles—you be the learner. Your child will learn by teaching you. These discussions could be held at the dinner table. But remember, they should be pleasant discussions. They are ways for you to keep track of where your child is in a chapter or in a learning unit. Perhaps you can use the questions at the end of the unit to direct these regular reviews. For example, your child might use them to quiz you, and then you could review the answers together. It is also helpful for your child to make up her own study questions about important ideas in a chapter. She could take them to the teacher. Who knows? The teacher might use these questions on a test.

6. Writing is an important way to learn. Help your child realize this by showing him how to organize

a notebook with a place for personal notes, a place for teacher handouts, and a place for assignments and tests. Such a notebook keeps all important study information in one handy place. When a chapter or unit of study is completed, encourage your child to write a two- or three-sentence summary. A brief summary will help give him a sense of closure by including the topic and answers to what, how, and why. For example, a chapter on the environment might be summarized with these two sentences: "The air we breathe will stay clean only if we all do our part. We need to use less gasoline and plant more trees in our cities to help nature recycle the air." As you can see, a summary acts only as a quick reminder of the chapter's content. The memory will then recall some of the important details.

If you remember to have homework become a regular part of your family's schedule and keep your discussions about homework as relaxed as possible, you can make major strides in using daily home learning in a beneficial way. You will soon see that by helping your child apply school learning to the world around her, you will make learning interesting and real. So do all you can to use maps in order to point out things and places mentioned on television. Also use the stove and refrigerator at home to demonstrate science principles. Finally, regularly use reference books as sources of information. Your attention to a few of these simple things will make homework the productive activity that it is meant to be.

Questions about Homework and School

All parents have questions and need answers about their children. Here are some questions that other parents have asked concerning homework.

> ➤ **The older my son gets, the more disorganized he seems to be! How can I help him learn to organize his school work?**

As children move into the higher grades, teachers expect them to assume more responsibility for their own learning. This means that children need to develop a system for organizing their studying — and their time — so they can be successful. As a parent, you can help your older child learn how to organize schoolwork.

"If you fail to plan, you plan to fail," says the old adage. It's true. At the beginning of the school year, help your son plan how to handle schoolwork and other activities he is involved with outside of school. Make a point to ask, "When do you want to schedule your homework time?" Then have your child write down a schedule. You might share with your son how you get yourself organized. Do you make lists? Do you use a calendar? The same system may appeal to your child.

Once your child has a plan, help him learn how to carry it out. Although homework is your child's responsibility, you can show your support in many ways, such as the following:

- Respect your child's study time. That means no radio, no TV, no phone calls, no interruptions from friends coming to play.

- Work on your own projects near your son. You can pay bills, write letters, or read a book. You can create a sense that "we're all in this together."

- Help your child lay out a plan for accomplishing longer projects. Write out a schedule for accomplishing a big task. Breaking a big job down into small tasks not only helps him experience success, but avoids the frustration and stress that comes with trying to do too much in too little time.

➤ **It is difficult for my children to come home after school and begin their homework. What can I do to help them complete their assignments within a reasonable time?**

After a long day of school, some kids just can't sit still long enough to finish their homework. For your children, "divide and conquer" might be good advice.

First, set a schedule that allows for plenty of breaks. For instance, work for 15 or 20 minutes, and then take a 5-minute break.

Second, help your children break down their homework into manageable pieces. For example, in one session your child might work 15 math problems.

In the next, she might look up 10 vocabulary words.

Third, give your children some free time. You might promise to play a favorite game or read a special story or do something together once homework is finished.

Fourth, allow for individual flexibility within the limits you set. Perhaps your family has the rule that homework must be done before dinner. One child prefers to do homework right after school. The other spends an hour outside before studying. Letting your children choose when they do homework places the responsibility on them for getting it done within your limits. This type of arrangement gives everyone some say in how homework is completed.

❯❯ **My child's teacher frequently uses the phrase "learning styles" when she offers suggestions to parents about helping their child with school work at home. What does she mean by this?**

As a parent, you know many things that make your child unique. Whether it's a talent for music or a great sense of humor, all children have something that makes them special. Kids also learn in different ways. A person's learning style is the way in which that individual learns best. For most children, one of these three learning styles will be strongest:

1. **Visual learners** learn mainly through seeing things. They learn best when they can see a picture in their minds. If they see something, such as printed directions, pictures, lists, or maps, they can understand it better. They comprehend better when they read what is in a book rather than hearing someone read it to them.

2. **Auditory learners** learn mainly through hearing. They learn best by listening and responding verbally. They can tell you the answer even though they have only been listening.

3. **Kinesthetic learners** learn through their bodies. They learn best by handling, touching, and manipulating things. They are more movement-oriented and when they have to sit still, their bodies seem to "go to sleep." One way to involve them is to have them write their thoughts down.

All children use all methods of learning. And no single style of learning is appropriate for all children. As a parent, you can help your children develop a homework style that seems best suited to the way each child learns.

For instance, here are some homework methods you can suggest to help a visual learner:

- Write lists of spelling words and post them.
- Put up a map of the United States with state capitals highlighted.
- Make a time line of important dates.
- Create flash cards to study vocabulary words or to learn math facts.

The following methods will help an auditory learner:

- Make up poems, rhymes, or other memory cues. Repeat them aloud.
- Repeat spelling words aloud.
- Read important lessons aloud.
- Tape record important reading assignments, facts, information, and vocabulary and spelling lists so that your child can listen to them on tape.

Kinesthetic learners can use these homework tips:

- Move around while studying. Try reading aloud while standing up.
- Act out an important lesson from history or perform creative dramatics from a story.
- Use a finger to focus the eyes while reading a textbook.
- Write and draw diagrams or illustrations for those things worth remembering.

➢ **We help our son every evening with school work in some way—reading aloud, math facts, spelling words, and other school-related assignments. He still struggles in school, and his papers and tests show very little improvement. Could he have a learning disability? What can we do?**

What's it like to have a learning difficulty? The American Academy of Pediatrics suggests imagining "a distorted television picture caused by technical problems at the station. There is nothing wrong with the TV camera at the station or the TV set in your home. Something in the internal workings of the TV station prevents it from presenting a good picture."

Children with learning difficulties usually can see and hear just fine. The American Academy of Pediatrics says "the problem occurs in the brain after the eyes and ears have done their job."

Some famous and successful people have learning disabilities. For example, Olympic Gold Medal winners Greg Louganis and Bruce Jenner have reading

disorders. Einstein had difficulties with arithmetic as a child. There is no sure cure for a learning difficulty. But there are ways to help children cope with these problems.

First, don't automatically suspect that your child has a brain disorder just because he or she has difficulty with a school subject. He may merely lack the background or the training to handle it.

Second, most schools have specialized testing facilities available to them. Talk to your son's teacher to see if the teacher thinks special testing is needed.

Third, discuss the problem with your doctor or pediatrician. She may have a recommendation for you.

Fourth, many communities have learning clinics

that will test children and provide a diagnosis and a plan for you.

Activities for Fun and Learning

As parents, we are looking for activities that will benefit our children. Here are some activities for fun and learning that you can enjoy with your child.

Creature Features

Help your child make different sizes of cylinders and cones using various colors of construction paper. Go for a walk and collect several rocks of assorted sizes and shapes. Decorate with paper, markers, tempera paint, beads, buttons, and fabric, to make all kinds of animals, creatures, and objects. Then it may be fun to do some sorting—by color, shape, or size.

Predictions

Together, think about what the world will be like in the future. Will we live on another planet? Do you think our lives will be dominated by computers? Decide on a time in the future, twenty or fifty years from now. Help your child write down some of her thoughts and predictions about the future world. Keep what she writes in a safe place, and when she grows older your child can read her forecasts to see if any of them came true.

Twisters

Choose either the first or last letter of your name. Make up sentences in which each word starts with that letter.

Claire can cut cantaloupe.
Bob buys big, blue, bus bumpers.
Mandy makes marvelous, mushy marshmallows.

If you repeat your sentence quickly, you will make your own tongue-twister.

These activities are from *My Own Fun,* by Carolyn Buhai Haas and Anita Cross Friedman (Chicago Review Press). This sourcebook is full of activities for parents to do with their children, ages seven through twelve.

Books for Parents

Homework without Tears, by Lee Canter and Lee Hausner. Presents a program to provide parents with an organized approach to helping their children with homework. Helps develop the skills to create a positive and stress-free learning environment in the home.

How to Help Your Child with Homework, by Marguerite C. Radencich and Jeanne Shay Schumm. Includes charts, resources, games, and study tools to help parents assist their children with homework. Topics include reading, spelling, writing, math, science, social studies, reports, and tests.

The Survival Guide for Kids with LD: Learning Differences, by Gary Fisher and Rhoda Cummings. A handbook which discusses learning differences and some school programs that are designed to help children manage them. Suggests ways to help children deal with learning disabilities, make friends, and cope with negative feelings. Includes a list of resources and organizations for kids.

Books to Read Together

Ages 6–8
Help Is on the Way for: Study Habits, by Marilyn Berry. Defines studying and explains why it is

important. Identifies three practical steps to help organize study time, space, and action plan. Gives suggestions to cope with study problems.

Study Smarts: How to Learn More in Less Time, by Judi Kesselman-Turkel and Franklynn Peterson. Proposes ways to streamline studying. Covers setting goals, taking notes, and decreasing review and reading time. Provides tips for special problems.

Ages 8–10

You Can Speak Up in Class, by Sara Gilbert. Addresses feelings of discomfort and anxiety that students have when speaking in the classroom. Presents reasons for the problems and gives practical ways to deal with them.

Tracking the Facts: How to Develop Research Skills, by Claire McInerney. Covers selecting a topic, using the library, interviewing, and computer searching. Also provides information on taking notes, organizing an outline, and writing up the research results.

Books for Children to Read by Themselves

Ages 6–8

What to Do When Your Mom or Dad Says...."Do Your Homework!" (and Schoolwork), by Joy Wilt Berry. Explains why children are given homework and the benefits of doing homework. Gives suggestions on how to do homework well and learn from it.

What to Do When Your Mom or Dad Says..."Get Good Grades!", by Joy Wilt Berry. Defines the purpose of tests and grades. Presents practical skills that will enable students to get the most out of tests and grades.

Ages 8–10

How to Be School Smart, by Elizabeth James and Carol Barkin. Examines different learning styles. Suggests ways to get organized. Includes chapters on homework and tests.

How to Write a Great School Report, by Elizabeth James and Carol Barkin. Guides the student through the different steps of writing a report. Outlines choosing a topic, finding information, taking notes, preparing to write, writing, editing, and proofreading.

7

Fitness and School Achievement

You may wonder how the condition of the body can affect learning, but there is no question that it does. Studies show that children who exercise regularly perform better in their school work than children who are not physically fit.

We Americans spend a lot of time thinking about fitness and health. You may be one of those people who has an exercise routine or who deliberately participates in activities that get you out and moving. You may even be one of those people that some folks call a "health nut." Whether you are or not, you may have given little or no thought to what fitness can do to your child's learning in school. You may have given even less thought to your role in your child's fitness. It's worth thinking about.

Fitness

When experts use the term fitness, they are referring to the ability of the body to supply oxygen to the muscles and the ability of the muscles to use oxygen efficiently for work. If oxygen is plentiful and our muscles use oxygen well while we are working or playing, we have the energy we need to do our work well. This healthy exchange of oxygen is developed through regular exercise, enough rest, and healthy food. Without sufficient exercise, our lungs and muscles do not develop the capacity for good oxygen exchange.

Then we are likely to feel tired or sluggish. If we don't get enough rest, we prevent our muscles from replenishing their needed oxygen, and of course we are still tired. Healthy food replaces the energy sources and vitamins and minerals that our body uses during work. If we stuff ourselves with fat and sugar (junk food), our body lacks the ingredients it needs to keep its muscles and organs working efficiently.

Why should you be concerned as a parent? Because you are the role model for your child. Especially in her early years, your child shapes her vision of how she should act from what she sees you do. If you walk or jog or swim, your child learns early in life that fitness activity is what important people do—because you are so important to your child. And just as exercise is important to your own self-concept, exercise also aids the self-concept of your child. Research shows clearly that children's self-concept can be increased by increasing their physical fitness. The reason a good self-concept is important in this discussion is that there is a strong relationship between a positive self-concept and good achievement in school. So that's one important way that fitness influences school achievement. If you feel energetic, and you think you look good because you are fit, you tend to perform your school work better.

This issue of fitness and self-concept is especially important for children who tend to be too heavy for their age. In one study, when students were asked to rate body types, the muscular body received the highest rating and the fat body the lowest. Children were asked to put labels on body types and they said that fat children were "stupid," "dirty," "lazy," and "smelly." Just from that study you can understand how a person's self-concept might be damaged by his physical appearance.

People with a weight problem often fall into a vicious cycle. As their weight increases, their desire for physical activity decreases; yet one of the key ingredients in weight control is physical activity. Most people must exercise to keep body fat under control. A balanced diet also is a factor. But quite often obese children and normal children eat the same number of calories each week. The difference is that normal children engage in much more physical activity. So set the example for your children and try to find ways that you can exercise together.

When your children are young, you can walk together, or jog if you prefer. Find games or recreation where your family has to move around to participate, such as shooting baskets, throwing a ball to one another, walking instead of riding to the store, bowling, playing tennis, or any number of active games. They can all be part of your effort to have fun, build your child's self-concept, and develop the energy base your child needs to perform well in school.

Nutrition

We live in a fast-food world—a world that encourages us to eat quickly and to eat food that doesn't take much time to prepare. You know, of course, that vegetables, meat, fish, and fruit in balanced meals give the kind of nutrition your body requires. And we know that in the hurried business of our lives, we would much rather grab and run than take the time to prepare or to order and eat a balanced meal. Part of the answer for a family is to make meal preparation a family activity.

If you have the space, you might grow a small home garden. That garden can give you some of the vegetables that you need for sandwiches and cooked meals. Even in a small plot you can grow tomatoes, lettuce, carrots, and zucchini. The garden provides movement and activity for everyone, and the use of those foods can get everyone involved in the preparation of some meals even if it is only cutting up carrots to put into each person's lunchbox.

There are always things that young children can do and will enjoy doing in the kitchen, for example, making biscuits from the many cut-and-bake products that can be purchased at the supermarket. Naturally, your children can help you mix and bake if you make everything from scratch.

Other ways that you can promote fitness at home include encouraging your school to develop a strong physical fitness program, reading about fitness to your child, or going with the entire family to a skating rink, a bowling alley, or a golf course. Schools often provide family fitness opportunities. Don't be afraid to get involved. Go to the school gym once a week and work out with other parents and children. As part of the President's Physical Fitness program, some schools issue an exercise calendar. Each day the family can perform an exercise routine. At the end of the month, when all the days have been marked with the parent's signature, the child receives a certificate of achievement.

Schools also offer nutrition programs from time to time. These discussions will remind you of the need to pay attention to your family's diet and also give you good ideas on how to provide your family with appetizing meals that are healthy, too. Look for information in your school newsletters. They may remind you to give after-school snacks that are nutritious, such as carrots, grapes, peanuts, and so on. They may also give a list of library books about eating habits. Here are a few examples:

- *Bread and Jam for Frances,* by Russell Hoban
- *Dandelion: The Lion Who Lost His Roar,* by Rose Stain
- *Old McDonald Had an Apartment House,* by Judith Barrett
- *Blueberries for Sal,* by Robert McCloskey

As a last reminder, make meals and exercise a pleasant time for the family to get together. In the long run, you and your children will cherish the pleasant times you had when you worked together to stay fit through exercise and eating well.

Please don't forget your child's need for a good night's sleep. Many teachers today worry about the tired children who fall asleep in school each day. They are the ones who have stayed up to watch late movies or other television programs. The average child seems to need about eight hours of sleep to function well on school tasks. Some need more, some a little less. As early in the life of your child as possible, start a bedtime routine that will calm your child and put him in the mood to sleep. Try to get on a schedule where bedtime is about the same time each night. Perhaps reading a story together, listening to soothing music, or talking about the good things that happened that day will ease your child into slumber.

You are important to your children. Give them the example and the direction of regular exercise, healthy diet, and plenty of daily rest. That's a good base for their work in school, work that is often difficult and requires their best energy.

Questions about Fitness and Health

Most parents are concerned about their children's diet, fitness, and general health. Here are answers to a few of the more common questions parents ask about these issues.

> **Our children participate in various sports throughout the year. Because of their interest in these different sports, we spend much of our time driving our children to games and practices, often times in different directions. What can we do for family recreation that involves everyone in our family at one time?**

Since your children's activities take you away from the home so much, you may want to consider ways your family can enjoy time together at home. We sometimes misinterpret the word recreation to mean only physical activity. Recreation is a means of refreshment or a diversion from our everyday jobs and routines. It is important that we give ourselves opportunities to enjoy our families in relaxing ways.

Reading can be refreshing and stimulating for us, as well as a way of relaxing at home with our families. Reading and sharing books at home—whether it's a favorite novel, a magazine, or the Sunday paper—can bring parents and children together. Set aside time for your family in which everyone can read and share books for pleasure. Family reading and talking about books not only increases family literacy, but it makes reading an interactive and social activity for your family.

> ⇒ **I am a single parent with two active boys. It isn't always possible for me to let them do everything they would like to, especially the more expensive activities such as basketball camps, overnight camping trips, weekend skiing, and so forth. Do you have suggestions for making our recreation affordable?**

Libraries and museums are still the best bargains around. Libraries usually offer programs year-round that are absolutely free—you just have to show up. The topics vary, and the programs are generally for a variety of interests and age levels. Many libraries have story hours, puppet plays, guest speakers and performers, and a variety of special activities throughout the year. Some libraries put out a monthly schedule or calendar of events. Others may put notices in local newspapers about upcoming library programs and activities. Take your family to your local library and check out what they have to offer.

The library can also be a good source for trying to find a hobby or recreation that your family can enjoy together. Your local library can provide you with books and information on a variety of recreation or hobby

ideas. Encourage your family to read about different types of recreation and share ideas about what would be enjoyable for everyone. Doing a little family re-search—finding out what recreation is available, what will suit your family interests, and what is afford-able—can lead you to recreation that everyone has had a part in selecting and will enjoy doing together.

Visiting museums is another inexpensive way to spend free time. Some museums are free, while others may ask for a donation or family pass that can be purchased and used year round. Museums, especially children's museums, offer special programs on a variety of topics. Many of these programs have hands-on type activities. Check to see if you need to pre-register your children for these programs. The exhibits and activities in museums change frequently, so there is always some-thing new, interesting, and fun to offer your children.

Also, inquire about free concerts, plays, exhibits, and hobby shows in your area. The "recreation" or "leisure" section of newspapers can give you more ideas and ways to enjoy leisure time with your fam-ily—without spending a lot of money.

➢ **I am concerned about my son's weight problem. We have talked about eating**

balanced meals, and he really has made an effort to eat nutritious snacks when he comes home from school. I have encouraged him to be more active and get some exercise after school rather than always watching TV. My subtle hints haven't worked. What can I do without always seeming to nag at him?

It's no secret that kids today are less fit—and heavier—than ever before. Today, one in five elementary school children is too heavy. That's an increase of 54 percent in just one generation. Many doctors say kids are fatter because they watch more TV and

consume more junk food. Studies show that the kids who are the most fit watch the least television—just one or two hours weekly, compared with a national average of more than 25 hours.

So one way to help your child control or reduce fat is by turning off the television. Make a rule that no TV is watched until after dinner—and stick to it! Encourage your child to try more active pursuits instead of spending so much time in front of the tube. You might suggest that some kids come over to play outdoor activities such as kickball, tag, hide-and-seek, and other children's games. Some children need other children around to be more active.

You can also find ways to work out together. You might take a brisk morning or evening walk. If your son is older, you can try jogging together. Or you can all enroll in a fitness class. Whether it's aerobics or tennis, you'll all get fit and have fun. Finally, you can start an exercise program yourself. One national study found that if either parent exercised, children were less likely to be fat. If the mother exercised, the child's chance of fitness increased even more. Even if your child doesn't exercise with you, the model you set can pay off.

> **Our child has a difficult time staying in bed once he gets there. We start to bed at 8:00 or 8:30, but it usually stretches into 9:30 with all the trips back and forth to the bathroom, drinks, snacks, questions, and so forth. Many times it takes angry words to get him to stay in bed. What can we do to make bedtime a more pleasant time for all of us?**

Many children, and adults too, need time to unwind and quietly relax before actually going to sleep. Reading to your child before bedtime is an excellent way to help him relax. We have bedtime at our house set for 8:00 and a "lights out" time for 8:30. The children must be ready for bed by 8:00 and the additional half

hour is used to read and unwind before falling asleep.

Parents know that some children who are sent to get a book or allowed to read before bedtime often don't do it. They are distracted by other things. I suggest keeping some of your child's favorite books by your bed or easy chair. When he comes to you at bedtime for a quick hug and kiss, you can read to him without delay and relax together. I think both you and your child will actually look forward to bedtime with this new routine.

Recreation Activities

Improve your children's health and spend some fun time with them by trying some of the following activities. Discuss these activities with your children. Ask them to select two or three that they would enjoy. Don't try to do them all, just two that work for you.

Hit the Trail
Most kids like to snack, and enjoy making their own creations in the kitchen. Let them make something

nutritious to eat. Below are two recipes you can use. Some adult supervision may be required to oversee this activity, and younger children may need someone to read the recipes to them.

Recipe: Trail Mix
Mix any combination of granola cereal, peanuts, flaked coconut, raisins, dried dates, apricots, banana chips.

Recipe: Munch Cakes
Spread peanut butter or applebutter over a rice cake. Top with raisins or bananas slices.

Read to Relax
A quiet activity can help your child settle down before going to bed. Share a book with your child by reading to her or letting her read to you. Older children might enjoy reading one chapter each evening from a longer book and then sharing it with you.

Exercise or Televise?
Compare family members' daily exercise and television viewing by making a chart. Let your children record how many minutes or hours they spend watching television and how many exercising or doing active recreation. At the end of the week, compare television time versus active recreation time, and decide if your family needs more exercise and less television time.

Be a Sport
If your family does need to be more fit, choose a sport or exercise in which you would like to participate. Go to your local library and check out a book about the topic. Find out the rules of the game, health risks, and equipment needs.

Praise Be!
Be sure to give your children lots of encouragement and praise when they join in physical activities. Reward them for their participation, not just for their skill level or team victory.

Books for Parents

The following resources will give you more information on fitness and nutrition:

Foodworks: Over 100 Science Activities and Fascinating Facts that Explore the Magic of Food, by Mary Donev and others. Uses fun activities to explain the role of food in our daily lives. Explores different kinds of foods, where they come from, and how the body uses those foods for fuel. Also covers vitamins, taste buds, and food recycling.

Dr. Eden's Healthy Kids, by Dr. Alvin N. Eden. Uses the latest findings on cholesterol, salt, sugar, and essential minerals to discuss exercise, nutrition, and obesity. Suggests diet and nutrition plans and exercise programs for children from infant through adolescent age. Includes healthy recipes for kid's favorite foods, tips to prevent iron deficiency and exercises to build cardiovascular strength.

The Complete Guide to Family Fitness Fun, by Dr. Charles T. Kuntzleman. Provides ideas to keep family members' cholesterol and weight at healthy levels. Lists fun activities to do as a family. Gives ways to prevent and control high blood pressure and stress. Presents charts on calories, cholesterol, caffeine, fast food, heart rates, and minerals and vitamins. Also includes recipes for healthy meals and snacks and exercise programs.

Books to Read Together

Ages 4–6

Dinosaurs Alive and Well! A Guide to Good Health, by Laurie Krasny Brown and Marc Brown. Some fun-loving dinosaurs show how to dress, eat well, relax, exercise the body and mind, and deal with feelings, worries, and stress. Includes tips on first-aid, a list of grown-ups to turn to for help, and some ideas to help prepare for sleep.

When We Went to the Park, by Shirley Hughes. A little girl and her grandpa go to the park to watch the daily activities. Children and adults are running, jogging, playing ball, and feeding the animals.

Ages 6–8

The Bicycle Man, by Allen Say. It is sports day at a small village school in Japan. The students compete for prizes and the parents join in the festivities also. Two American soldiers share in the fun when they borrow the principal's bicycle to perform some stunts.

The Healthy Habits Handbook, by Slim Goodbody. A guide to developing healthy habits. Covers posture, nutrition, breathing, safety, and sleep. Includes tips for home and school.

Ages 8–10

Fred's TV, by Clive Dobson. Fred is a TV addict. He isn't playing ball anymore or running around outside with his friends. They all prefer to watch TV and eat during their free time. One day Fred's dad decides to destroy the TV. Fred is in terrible shape until he converts the TV into a bird feeder. Now Fred is active again and has a hobby as well.

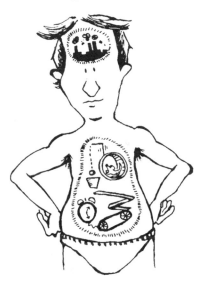

Bodyworks: The Kids' Guide to Food and Physical Fitness, by Carol Bershad and Deborah Bernick. Explains how the body works and uses the food we eat. Looks at lifestyles in general, eating habits, nutrition, exercise, and food selection.

Books for Children to Read by Themselves

Ages 4–6

What Happens When You Sleep? by Joy Richardson. Explains why people need sleep and what happens during sleep. Touches on dreams, snoring, relaxation, eye movement, and sleeping positions.

Wait, Skates! by Mildred D. Johnson. A little boy gets a new pair of skates, but they just won't wait for him. His skates go all directions, and so does he.

He practices skating until his skates can wait and he can skate straight.

Ages 6–8

Clara's Dancing Feet, by Jean Richardson and Joanna Carey. Clara loves to dance, as long as she is at home. She decides to go to class, but feels she can't dance in front of people. Clara gets over being shy and discovers she is able to perform with the rest of her class.

Jam, by Margaret Mahy. Mr. Castle doesn't want to waste the fruit from the family's plum tree, so he makes plum jam. Day after day he makes plum jam until every container in the house is filled with jam. The Castle family eats jam all year until they are sick of jam and chubby from eating so much of it. They discover what "too much of a good thing" means.

Ages 8–10

Keeping in Shape, by Nancy Lewis and Richard Lewis. A guide to exercise and physical fitness. Includes an exercise program based on recommendations of the American Alliance for Health, Physical Education, and Recreation.

Good for Me! by Marilyn Burns. Explores good food and bad food, the digestive system, nutrition and malnutrition, and vitamins. Gives short stories about foods we eat, such as the creation of hamburgers and how potato chips were invented.

Working with the School

We hear lots of talk these days about parent involvement in schools and in their children's education. In fact, the phrase "parent involvement" is used so often that it's worth asking just what it means.

Recently, while flying to a meeting, I told the person sitting next to me that I wrote articles for a parent magazine. He immediately started talking about his children and his concern about their education. He said that some of his friends were teaching their children at home and were not sending them to school. He and his wife were not going to set up their own home school. But they were interested in how they could work with their local school to give their children the tools they needed to succeed in life.

What a wonderful, positive attitude this man had

about parent involvement! He wanted to work with the school to help his children gain the information, skills, and creative expression they needed to succeed as learners and responsible citizens. I think that's an excellent definition of parent involvement. It suggests that parents should focus on their children's learning and share decisions and responsibilities with teachers and other school personnel.

By concentrating on what your children are learning, you have something to discuss at parent-teacher conferences. Besides the general question of whether or not they are doing okay, you can ask specifically what they are able to do as readers, writers, scientists and mathematicians. Since you share with the school the responsibility of helping your children make progress and develop a positive attitude toward learning, you and the teacher need to talk about specific plans that will help your children achieve these goals.

Your efforts to carry out a plan for your children usually center around homework and a place for home study. You need to provide a regular study time, a place to study away from TV and other distractions, resource books, such as grammar handbooks, and your own time. We can't lose sight of the value of homework in individual learning. Showing your interest in your children's school work and in helping them at home contributes significantly to their success in school. Researcher Joyce Melton has found that parents' daily interest in school and school learning contributes more to children's success than does simply participating in conferences or volunteering to work at school.

Of course, volunteering to work at school or in your child's classroom is a beneficial way for you to get involved. Whether you work on a PTO project or tutor children at school, once you are there, you have easy access to the teachers, principals, and counselors who can also help you with your own child's education.

Parent involvement may also include becoming an advocate for your child and for other children in the school. This may mean that you take an individual complaint to the principal and ask for the legal channels which protect the interests of a group of children. Your attention to these problems helps schools focus attention on these children. For example, there may be a group of families who don't speak English well and for whom the school needs a policy change to help them succeed in school.

Another aspect of the home-school picture is your own continuing education. Because we are always discovering new things about how children learn, we are regularly adjusting the school curriculum to meet new needs, such as, drug and AIDS education. By going to information meetings, seminars, and health demonstrations you may become better informed about the techniques that schools currently use. This kind of information can guide you in assisting your own children.

Your interest has significant benefits. From various studies of parent involvement in education we know that parental concern leads to improved children's school achievement and self-esteem. Just having Mom or Dad show an interest in their world gives children a boost, a sense of importance.

Parents also help themselves. Working together with school personnel improves parents' self-worth—perhaps because they acquire useful skills that can be used with their children and because they begin to realize how valuable they are to their children.

At any rate, when it comes to parent involvement, "just do it," as one ad campaign tells us. Your kids will benefit, you will benefit, and the school will be a better place for children because one more adult has contributed to its mission. A couple of years ago, I had the pleasure of visiting twenty-three highly successful schools. One common factor in each was a high degree of parent involvement.

What should you do? Here are some things you can do to make sure your relationship with your child's school will help her:

1. Focus your discussions on your child, not on the teacher or school. How can we work together to benefit the child?
2. Include the principal and school counselor when your child needs their attention, too.
3. Insist that teachers and other school personnel talk everyday language. If someone uses educational jargon, ask for an explanation that you can understand.

4. Share your first-hand experiences about your child and her needs.

5. By all means, disagree with a teacher's comments if your experience counters what he or she says. Create a dialogue about your child.

6. Let your child know that you will work at home to support efforts started in the classroom. You and the teacher will work together to help your child achieve success. Don't engage in "teacher bashing."

7. Build a collaborative attitude between yourself and the school. When you think of school personnel who can help you with your child, remember that there are many people who will work with you— principal, counselor, nurse, social worker, coach, music teacher, and so on. Get to know them, and ask for their assistance when it is needed.

8. If your child has a problem at school, sometimes a conflict between you and school professionals may arise. Take the attitude that you can negotiate your differences because you both have the goal of improving your child's education.

These suggestions will make relationships between you and the school, you and your child, and your child and the school, beneficial to all involved.

Parents' Questions about School

Parents often ask questions about interactions with the school. Here are some examples:

➤ **I'm a single father. Do you have any suggestions for me and other parents who would like to volunteer to do things at school, but find it difficult because of work schedules?**

Even though you are very busy, there are still ways you can participate in school. One father I know uses his personal holiday one day a year to help in his son's class. He eats lunch with his son and spends the afternoon watching and helping in the class.

Young children feel honored when a parent visits their classroom to help. Some businesses establish close relationships with schools in their community and encourage home-school communication by allowing parents time off to attend parent-teacher conferences.

Some schools invite parents for lunch. They set aside certain days of the month when parents can join their children at school for lunch. Notices are sent home reminding parents of the dates. Parents must notify the school ahead of time so that the cafeteria can prepare extra lunches. Check your school's lunch policy. If it doesn't offer such an invitation, it might be that the idea never occurred to school officials. Perhaps you could get a parents' lunch day started.

Parents can volunteer to talk to a class about their jobs, special interests, or hobbies. A parent of one of my students worked for a railroad. We were studying a unit on transportation, so on his visit to school he talked about trains, their design, how they have changed over the years, and how they benefit our state. He discussed train safety and involved the children in a lively discussion. Later, he arranged a field trip for us to visit the train depot where he worked. There are details about every job that would prove interesting to curious young minds. Check with your child's teacher to see if you can share your interests and expertise with his class.

There are many activities going on outside the classroom that support the school. For example, banquets, plays, carnivals, book fairs, sports, and other events are organized by teacher and parent groups. The principal's office can help you find an activity that best suits your schedule and interests.

Remember that parent involvement doesn't always mean being visible in the school. Helping your

child at home with school work, taking time to read aloud, and doing other school-related activities are important contributions to your child's education. Many teachers ask parents to spend time each evening working on math or reading with their child. This may be the best way to show your support.

➤ **I don't like to attend parent-teacher conferences. I usually sign up for a conference time and then don't show-up. Are parent-teacher conferences really that important?**

Psychologist James Comer says that to get the best education, children need to have a team behind them. At a minimum, this team is made up of parents and teachers working together. Children who are well behaved and working on grade level need this team support just as much as those with learning difficulties, those who are unmotivated, or those who lack self-discipline.

Perhaps you back out of school conferences because you lack the self-confidence to face a teacher about your child. It may seem silly to you but it is a good idea to dress up for a conference like you would if you were going to work in an office. Dressing like a professional may add to your self-confidence.

It is also a good idea for both parents to attend the conference. If you are divorced or separated, of course this may not be possible. When both parents go to the conference they act as a team and support one another on important issues.

Go into the conference with a written list of questions and concerns. The teacher will appreciate your interest and preparation. Don't be afraid to ask a lot of questions. This is your child's education you're talking about. Press the teacher for ways in which you can all work together to benefit your child.

❯ I always go to my children's parent-teacher conferences, but feel very uneasy and "draw a blank" when their teachers ask if I have any questions. Do you have any advice for an interested, but nervous, parent?

School conferences are great ways for parents and teachers to learn more about children. You can make your conference more successful if you do some "homework" first. Many of us are better at asking questions when we think in advance of what we want to ask.

Here are questions you may want answered:

- What are my child's strengths and weaknesses?

- What are my child's work habits like?
- Does my child need extra help in any subject?
- Are there things we can do at home to help her?
- Is my child making normal progress in reading? In math?
- Does my child complete homework regularly?
- How does my child relate to other children? To other adults?

Besides asking about your child's school work, you need to share information that can help the teacher know and understand your child. Be sure to tell the teacher about health needs, your child's interests, or any changes in your home or family that affect your child's learning. The most important thing to remember about a conference is to attend it. Just by being there you show the teacher and your child that you are interested in their work. That goes a long way toward building a cooperative spirit among you.

➤ How can I develop good communications with my children's teachers?

The most important point to remember in developing an open line of communication with your children's teachers is don't wait for the first conference. Find time within the first couple of weeks of school to meet your children's teachers. If you have any special concerns, make sure teachers are aware of them. Perhaps your child has vision or hearing problems that require special seating. Make sure your child's teacher is aware of his special needs.

Let teachers know where you can be reached during the day, and that you would appreciate being contacted should problems arise. From that point on, whenever you sense that your child is having a problem in school, call her teacher immediately. When parent-teacher conference time arrives, there should be no surprises.

➣ **My son has attended a school for handicapped children. This year he will be mainstreamed into a regular public school classroom. We want this to be a positive experience. What can we do to support the school's efforts in this situation?**

Become an educated parent. Find out all you can about the nature of your child's disability and how it affects school performance. Ask teachers and other professionals for reading material, and go to the public library for information. This will help you avoid making unrealistic demands for academic achievement on both your child and his teacher.

Have realistic expectations about what the school can and cannot do. Join a parent support group or parent-teacher organization that will help you determine if the school is effective in helping your child. There may also be a national organization linking families concerned about a particular handicap. Such organizations are excellent sources of information and support.

Work closely with your child's teacher. Being in a regular classroom is a new experience for your child. Keep in close touch with the teacher, and see how you can help. Make sure you understand the terminology your child's teacher uses to describe your child's unique needs. Often times such terms are clear

to teachers who use them frequently, but not clear to parents. Don't be afraid to ask questions, to ask for further explanations, or even to seek another opinion.

Don't assume the school can do everything without your assistance. Find out what the school is doing and what strategies are being used. Perhaps there are things you can do at home that will reinforce school activities. Keeping in close contact strengthens the parent-teacher team. If you are having a problem with your child at home, alert the school. Teachers or school officials may have suggestions to make, and can tell you if the problem is interfering with school performance. Keep a positive attitude. It will help your child.

If a teacher contacts you about problems with your child, try not to be defensive. First, listen to his side of the story. No matter how difficult this might seem, think of it as an opportunity to share information and ideas. When you show that you are concerned with what a teacher or administrator is saying, he will be more willing to listen when you have the floor. When a problem arises, suggest a meeting so you can address the problem together. Face-to-face discussions are much more effective than trying to solve problems over the telephone.

Speaking positively about school or the teacher fosters a respectful attitude in your child, and can contribute to healthy school performance. A feeling of mutual respect and commitment between parent and teacher helps your child.

Take advantage of the invitations your school extends. Attend back-to-school night, parent-teacher conferences, and other school-related activities. Get together with other parents at PTO meetings or other parent support groups. Knowing what goes on at school can extend and enrich your child's school performance.

Contact the school frequently. Don't wait until a problem becomes serious before contacting the school. If your child seems unhappy or frustrated, contact the school immediately. Alert the teacher to problems you feel are significant. Many times minor problems can be solved before they reach crisis proportions if home and school have open lines of communication.

Try not to get angry if you find that the school does not include you in making decisions about your child to the degree you want. Anger often turns off those people who are in a position to help. Instead, restate clearly that the best approach to educating your child is if each party knows what the other is doing. This way neither parent nor teacher works against the other's efforts.

Books for Parents

Empowering Your Child, by D. Fred Bateman. Shows parents how to create a home environment that will stimulate their children's academic development and help them succeed in school. Deals with topics such as reading, trust, self-esteem, responsibility, discipline, family relationships, and study habits.

Staying Back, by Janice Hale Hobby. Presents the stories of seven children who repeated a grade, and later became successful students. Also gives guidance for parents trying to support their children through this experience.

I Hate School! Some Commonsense Answers for Parents Who Wonder Why, by Jim Grant. Discusses

school readiness, failure and retention, and developmental placement. Gives examples of sig-
nals children send when they need help.
Helping Your Child Achieve in School, by Dr. Barbara
Johnson. Deals with motivation, reading, testing, and beginning school. Also covers parents
and teachers as partners, gifted children, and
computers.

Index

Parents' Notes

Parents' Notes

From the Family Literacy Center . . .

Tapes and booklets* to accompany this book:

____ Learning and Self-Esteem (C05; $7)
____ Motivating Your Child to Learn (C04; $7)
____ Stress and School Performance (C14; $7)
____ Discipline and Learning (C06; $7)
____ Parents as Models (C13; $7)
____ Encouraging Good Homework Habits (C16; $7)
____ Recreation for Health and Learning (C09; $7)
____ Working with the School (C17; $7)

*Booklets include the information presented in this book
plus stories to read aloud or listen to with your child.

To order:

1. check off the topic(s) above
   that you are interested in
2. fill out the information below
3. send form with payment to:

   Family Literacy Center
   Indiana University
   2805 E. 10th St., Suite 150
   Bloomington, IN 47408-2698

Subtotal_____

IN Residents add
5% sales tax_____

Shipping_____

Total:_____

Shipping Charges: 1 bk: $2.00   4-7 bks: $4.00
                        2-3 bks: $3.00   8+ bks: $5.00

Name _____

Address _____

_____ Zip _____

Method of payment: ❏ Check   ❏ Money Order
                          ❏ VISA   ❏ MasterCard

Cardholder_____

Card Number _____

Expiration Date_____

❏ Please send me the Family Literacy Center catalog!

Special Offer!

Write or call now for your free year's
subscription to Grayson Bernard
Publishers' parent newsletter:

Parent & *Child . . . learning together*

Receive four quarterly issues filled with information
and advice all concerned parents need.

Simply mail in the order form below or call
(812) 331-8182 for your free subscription.

- - - - - - - - - - - - - - - - - - - -

Name _____

Address _____

City _____ Zip _____

Ages of my children _____

Topics I'd like to read about _____

Mail to: Grayson Bernard Publishers
             Free Subscription Offer
             P.O. Box 5247, Dept. P2
             Bloomington, IN 47407

From Grayson Bernard Publishers . . .

The Confident Learner: Help Your Child Succeed in School *Simic, McClain, Shermis*
A confidence builder for both parents and children!

Help Your Child Read and Succeed: A Parents' Guide *Carl B. Smith, Ph.D.*
Practical, caring advice with skill-building activities for parents and children.

Smart Learning: A Study Skills Guide for Teens *Dr. William Christen & Thomas J. Murphy*
Learn to focus study energies for fantastic results!

Elementary Grammar: A Child's Resource Book *Carl B. Smith, Ph.D.*
Handy source of answers for young learners and their parents.

Intermediate Grammar: A Student's Resource Book *Carl B. Smith, Ph.D.*
A student's grammatical lifesaver.

Look for these titles in your local bookstore.
Or order conveniently by telephone or mail.
See the next page for order information.

Order Information

☎ To order by phone, call toll-free **1-800-356-9315** and use your VISA, MasterCard, or American Express.

✉ To order books by mail, fill out the form below and send check or money order to:

Grayson Bernard Publishers
P.O. Box 5247, Dept. P2
Bloomington, IN 47407

Order Form

Qty.	Title	Author	Unit Cost	Total
	The Confident Learner	Simic, M.	$ 9.95	
	Help Your Child Read and Succeed	Smith, C.	$12.95	
	Smart Learning	Christen/ Murphy	$11.95	
	Elementary Grammar	Smith, C.	$13.95	
	Intermediate Grammar	Smith, C.	$16.95	

Shipping & Handling:
❏ Book Rate: $2.00 for the first book plus $1.00 for each additional book.
❏ Air Mail: $3.00 for the first book plus $1.50 for each additional book.

Subtotal	
Shipping & Handling	
IN residents add 5% sales tax	
Total	

Send books to:

Name _____

Address _____

_____ Zip _____

Prices subject to change.

Your satisfaction is guaranteed.
Any book may be returned within 60 days for a full refund.

Grayson Bernard Publishers is a publisher of books for families and educators dedicated to promoting literacy and educational achievement. Our primary goal is to provide quality resources for parents and children to enrich the home learning environment.

For more information about *The Confident Learner* or any of our publications, please contact us at:

Grayson Bernard Publishers
223 S. Pete Ellis Drive, Suite 12
P.O. Box 5247
Bloomington, IN 47407
(812) 331-8182

The **Family Literacy Center** at Indiana University was established to promote family involvement in literacy, which includes all kinds of family activities related to reading, writing, and general communication. The Center engages in research on family literacy, promotes activities and events that encourage family literacy, and sells and disseminates parent involvement materials.

To learn more about the Family Literacy Center, its programs and publications, contact:

Family Literacy Center
Indiana University
2805 E. 10th Street, Suite 150
Bloomington, IN 47408
(812) 855-5847